# GOLF SCHOOL

# GOLF SCHOOL

BY ALEX HAY AND
JULIAN WORTHINGTON

ALL TECHNIQUES DEMONSTRATED BY PAUL KENT

CHARTWELL
BOOKS, INC.

**A QUARTO BOOK**

Published by Chartwell Books Inc.,
A Division of Book Sales Inc.,
110 Enterprise Avenue,
Secaucus, New Jersey 07094

ISBN 1-55521-089-9



This book was designed and produced by
Quarto Publishing Limited
The Old Brewery
6 Blundell Street
London N7 9BH

Senior Editor: Stephen Paul
Designer: Pete Laws

Illustrator: Mick Hill
Photographers: Ian Howes, John Hesletine, Brent Moore

Art Director: Nigel Osborne
Editorial Director: Jim Miles



Typeset by Facsimile Graphics Limited, Coggeshall, England
Colour origination by Trinity Graphic Centre, Hong Kong
Printed by Lee Fung Asco Printers Ltd, Hong Kong

**Quarto Publishing would like to thank the La Manga Club, Costa Calida, Spain, for the generous loan of their superb golfing facilities for the location photography.**

# CONTENTS

# INTRODUCTION

The rapidly increasing popularity of golf as a pastime as well as a sport has much to do with the changes in social patterns in recent years. There is no doubt that extra leisure time and (for the more fortunate members of society) increased wealth have played a major part in changing the image of the game. This trend is evident not only in the growing number of people who now play, but also in the many who watch – either on the course itself or from the comfort of their homes.

New courses, both private and public, have provided much needed facilities for the growing golf-playing population and valuable opportunities for all wishing to take up the game – young and old, rich and not so rich. In addition, the incentives for younger players are better than ever before. There is now greater scope to play in tournaments not only at home but also abroad, and for the tireless professional the season can last virtually the whole year round.

Many golfers play just for fun, highlighting the obvious benefits of companionship, friendly rivalry and exercise, as well as a solution to filling in some of those hours of leisure. Here, in particular, golf has much to offer since it enables people of varying ability to go out and play together and compete on level terms.

The dangers of playing golf at this level, however, are all too obvious. Because it is possible as a high-handicap golfer to play against those of a much higher standard and compete at club level, the incentives to improve may not be as strong as they could be.

In this respect golf is no different to any other sport, where the object is always to play better and compete harder. This, after all, is the instinctive way of enjoying the game – and this should always be encouraged as a healthy motivation. For the average player, there is bound to be a limit to the improvement that can be achieved. No one is suggesting that in time everyone who takes up golf seriously should become a scratch player. But the target all players should set themselves is to aim to bring that handicap down and strive for their own personal level of achievement.

## Getting priorities right

If you want to get the most from your golf, you should never be satisfied by being mediocre all the time. There is nothing easier than playing your way around the course, rejoicing over a few lucky shots but accepting that most were inevitably modest and quite often bad. If you were honest with yourself, you can never really claim to have enjoyed the round. But worse than this, there will be times when the effect is positively destructive. Having sliced the ball into the rough or chipped short of the green into yet another bunker for the umpteenth time, you will quickly lose heart and your game will deteriorate even further.

Only the best players can expect to get it right most of the time, and rest assured even the top professionals cannot guarantee every shot they play. What they *have* learned, however, is to know what they should be doing and, when things do not work out as planned, where they are going wrong – this should be every golfer's objective.

There are many qualities that go to making a good golfer. Ability is the most obvious one, but there are others that, even without too much ability, could be developed to help you with your game. Of these, fitness is one of the most important not least because it is closely linked to concentration. The overall approach to the game in general, and each shot in particular, is one area that every would-be golfer should work hard at. This is why the mental aspects are so vital – thinking carefully about each shot, which club to use, where to play the ball, what the state of the ground is. You need plenty of patience when the ball just will not run for you and plenty of finesse when it comes to that awkward or delicate shot. Timing is critical, and a good sense of this is a major step toward mastery of the required techniques.

Less important, possibly, but equally a useful asset, is strength. As you will see when you read on, power in the shot is determined more by the quality of execution, including the timing, than physical strength. There will be times when shot selection may be determined by the physique and power of the player. Any advantages, however, tend to balance themselves out over the course of a round and do not handicap the weaker player to any extent.

## Learning the basics

You may be surprised to hear that golf is essentially a simple game. The better the player, the more the basic elements of golf can be developed; but this takes time and a great deal of practice. For the average player – and particularly for the beginner – the golden rule is *keep it simple*.

The vast majority of the problems experienced by the average golfer are self-inflicted. It is vital that you understand from the very beginning that bad habits are easy to develop and very difficult to get out of. The obvious solution is to avoid getting into them, so always go back to the basics when you find yourself in trouble. If you have learned these thoroughly you will find that most of your problems can be solved by concentrating on executing the basic techniques correctly.

Why are these basic techniques so vital to the game of golf? Because they concern all the elements of preparation for the shot, since virtually all the faults in the shots you play can be traced back to the stages prior to the strike. These include the setting-up procedure, the grip on the club and the development of the swing. Understanding these and practicing the right techniques will go a long way to making you a reasonable player.

As with any ball game, control is the key factor. In the case of golf, this means knowing in which direction the ball will travel, what kind of flightpath it will have and how far it will go. Often average club players sacrifice control because elements of their basic technique have gone wrong. If these techniques are not learned and practiced thoroughly, there is no way of tracing the cause of the problem or putting it right. In this situation every shot becomes a matter of guesswork and luck plays an ever-increasing role in where the ball goes.

Pool and tennis are good examples of this principle. In pool you must first learn the right cue action and how to hit the ball straight before you can hope to master the angled shot or put spin on the cue ball. The same is true for tennis. Until you have complete control over your racket and can play a clean forehand or backhand drive, you are wasting your time attempting the more complex volley or smash shots.

Your approach to golf should be exactly the same. Any attempt to play a delicate shot with a lofted iron or to control a hook shot around an obstacle that lies ahead of you will invariably end in failure if you cannot drive the ball reasonably straight with your standard shots, using irons and woods. The message is clear and obvious – *do not run before you can walk*. The more you concentrate on, and the better you perfect, the basic techniques, the easier and more successful the harder shots will be.

Ford
YATES

GOLF EXHIBITION
SELF DRIVE
Willhire
SATELLITE
Wilson
Schweppes '84

## Varying your game

One of the great joys of golf is the enormous variety of courses on which it can be played. Wherever you go, you are guaranteed a different set of holes, each with their own special characteristics and individual problems. Add to this the fact that the way any course plays will depend on the prevailing conditions at the time and you will quickly realize that golf offers a new challenge virtually every time you step onto a course, even when most of your golf is played over the same course.

Despite the many variables you will be confronted with, there are certain characteristics that typify particular courses and thus divide them into two basic categories – links and inland.

Links courses are among the oldest in the world and are regarded by some as the more traditional venue for golf. (Interestingly, the British Open championship is always played on a links course.) Links courses are strongly associated with Scotland, where arguably the game of golf as we know it was born. It is perhaps significant, therefore, that the game's governing body presides at the Royal and Ancient Golf Club at St Andrews in Fife, Scotland.

Links courses provide the greatest challenge to the golfer because they are natural strips of land bordering the sea and are consequently exposed to all the elements. The ground is often sandy and the turf short and coarse, so the lie of the ball is usually very tight. Coastal vegetation in the form of gorse and heather can pose a real threat to the wayward golfer who misses the fairway. In addition, the greens on this type of course are generally very fast and often undulating.

Inland courses, on the other hand, present a different challenge. Since they are purpose built, with specially designed man-made hazards, the contest is more one of golfer versus course architect. The grass is generally richer and softer and the often uniformly flat greens on the whole slower, making the outcome of pitch shots more predictable. The skill needed is not so much to cope with the elements as to avoid the problems awaiting the unsuspecting player in the form of bunkers and ponds, as well as trees and bushes on and around the fairway.

In both cases, playing can be a memorable experience. On the links courses the marine views are interesting and at times rugged and spectacular, while inland the richness and grandeur of the scenery cannot fail to impress. Naturally your mind should be concentrating on the shot in hand, but when that does go astray there is always some compensation to be had in admiring the surrounding scenery.

## Keeping in practice

It is a mistake to think that simply playing a round or two of golf regularly will automatically improve your game. More often than not it will only perpetuate any faults you have developed until they eventually become a permanent feature of your game. You should remember that once on the course you must pay due consideration to other golfers waiting to play their round. Do not waste time by practicing a particular shot or, which is just as bad, stand around discussing it afterwards.

The time to practice is between rounds, and it is very important that you approach this with a positive attitude. There is little point in swinging away aimlessly for hours on end. Concentrate on a particular technical aspect – whether it be your stance or a part of your swing – or the use of a particular club. A half-hour's serious practice is worth a great deal more than hours of uncoordinated slogging, for not only does the practice have no purpose, but tired limbs will only aggravate the situation and do more harm than good to your golf.

Even with short periods of practice you can easily become bored, so set yourself targets and vary these to provide a constant challenge. You can make your life a lot easier – and the practice more effective – if you select the ground carefully. There is no point in playing off a bad lie if you want to develop a sound swing and hit the ball straight. Deliberately practicing awkward shots is, of course, another matter.

One very important aspect of practicing to eliminate faults is to seek the advice of a club teaching professional. Very often you may not be in a position – or have the experience – to identify exactly where you are going wrong. Then is the time to speak to an expert, so that you can be put right at an early stage. This does not mean that your tutor has to stand over you. If you take regular tuition, once he is familiar with your swing, a few words of advice may be all that is required to clarify a particular point or iron out a nagging problem.

## Getting started

The road to mastering the basic technique of golf or improving your existing game is not an easy one. Only you can decide how seriously you wish to be a better golfer. The guidelines laid down in this book have been arranged to lead you progressively through the essential stages of the game, and it cannot be stressed too strongly that the order of priorities is crucial if progress is to be made.

You may feel that your basic game is quite satisfactory, but that you want to improve on your spin shots or your play from bunkers. Before you rush to those particular sections, spend some time running through the basic techniques. It could just be that your swing is not quite as perfect as it should be and does not provide you with any sound foundation from which to adapt for specialist shots. And that might well be the answer to the problems you are having with spin shots or your bunker play.

Particularly for those starting from scratch, do not be in too much of a hurry to get out on the course. The more time you spend developing your technique, the better the results when you do go out for a round and the better equipped you will be to cope with the inevitable crises you find yourself in.

Finally a word to all left-handed players. To simplify the instructions in this book, the various techniques have been discussed and illustrated as for right-handed golfers. Left-handed players should simply reverse these instructions where appropriate.

5

SECTION ONE

# CHOOSING EQUIPMENT

The market for golf equipment and accessories has become big business. Professional's shops at clubs, which are also open to nonmembers, often look more like fashion showrooms, with every conceivable extra on sale. Your own budget will determine what you can buy, but even if you have plenty of money to spend you should still be wary and choose carefully.

In terms of equipping yourself to play golf, the arguments are the same as for any other pastime. There is no point in getting more than you need to start off with until you have really decided that golf is your sport. At the same time you want to make sure that everything you do buy is going to be used enough to justify the expenditure. But, most important of all, you must insure that what you buy is right for you, suits your physique and style of play and actually helps rather than hinders your own game.

This is particularly important when you come to choose your clubs. It is far better to hire – or, if you can, borrow – a few clubs to get the feel of them before you commit yourself to buying your own. Since they are a relatively expensive item, you will be less than happy if you discover, after buying a new set, that the weight or length, for example, is not right. Although certain modifications can be made to golf clubs, these will involve you in additional and unnecessary expenditure. It is far better to buy the correct type of clubs first time. The person to give you the best advice is the club professional, who can prove over the years to be a trusted ally, friend and adviser.

FREQUENCY-MATCHED
FREQUENCY MATCHED
PING

## The clubs

Golf clubs are divided into two main categories – woods and irons – which have traditionally been given some wonderful names. Despite the fact that both the woods and the irons are now numbered in sequence to distinguish the angle of loft on the club-face, many of these names have survived and are still sometimes referred to.

**Driver** The name of this wood is one that has survived, although its modern equivalent – the No.1 wood – has more than double the loft angle, making it easier to use.

**Brassie** With the original small loft angle on the driver, this wood used to be quite popular. Its equivalent – the No.2 wood – is not often used today since the modern No.1 wood has a similar loft angle.

**Spoon** This is the equivalent of the No.3 wood, whose capacity for hitting long shots has made it the most popular wood for the fairway.

**Baffie** Today this wood is represented by the No.4 and No.5 woods, which are much easier to use because of their greater swing weight and loft angle – up to 25 degrees – as well as a shorter length of shaft. With these you can lift the ball quite quickly, making them ideal when playing out of rough grass, provided that you have a reasonable lie.

**Driving iron** This is now represented by the No.1 or No.2 iron. Although used by professionals who are looking more for accuracy than distance, these irons are not recommended for beginners since, with a loft angle of between 14 and 18 degrees, a very accurate swing is needed.

**Long iron** The equivalent modern irons are the No.3 and No.4, which are used when playing from the fairway to the green depending, of course, on the distance.

**Mashie** The No.5 and No.6 irons have taken the place of the mashie. With their greater loft angles, they are particularly useful when playing from the semi-rough.

**Mashie niblick** This was a very useful iron, which has been replaced by the No.7 and No.8. Both will help you get height and distance into the shot.

**Niblick** This used to have the greatest loft angle. The modern replacements would be the No.9 iron and the pitching wedge, which are ideal for getting out of or over trouble since you can make the ball rise very quickly. The sand iron, which has a loft angle of 58 degrees, will do a similar job in a bunker.

**Putter** Original designs did have a slight loft angle on the club-face simply to cope with the rougher greens. Since these are now – or should be – as smooth as a billiard table, there is virtually no loft angle on the putters, the idea being to roll the ball across the surface and not lift it at all.

The basic reason for instituting a numbering system for woods and irons was to provide intermediate clubs in the range so that better players, in particular, could have the means of bridging the distance gap between the traditional clubs. Within a full set of clubs, there is a gap of about 3m (10ft) between each one which enables the golfer to select the most suitable club for the distance he or she needs to carry.

The maximum number of clubs allowed in a full set is 14. Although the exact composition will vary according to the golfer, the average player would probably select the following: woods – Nos. 1, 3, 4 and 5; irons – Nos. 3, 4, 5, 6, 7,

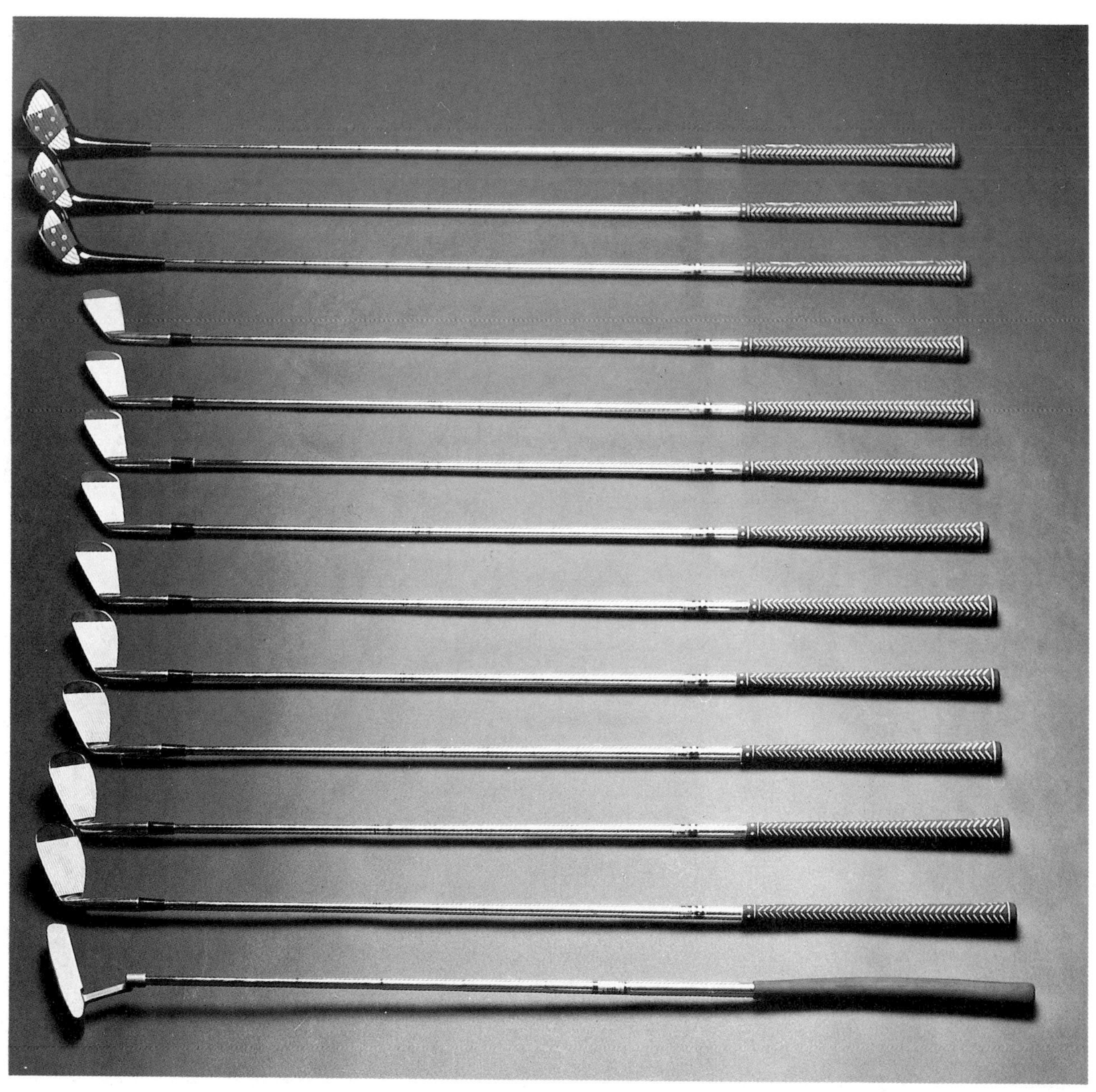

*This set of men's clubs (ABOVE) includes (from top to bottom) the following: driver and Nos. 3 and 5 woods; Nos. 3–9 irons; pitching wedge; sand iron; and Ping putter. To complete the set, you could add a No.4 wood.*

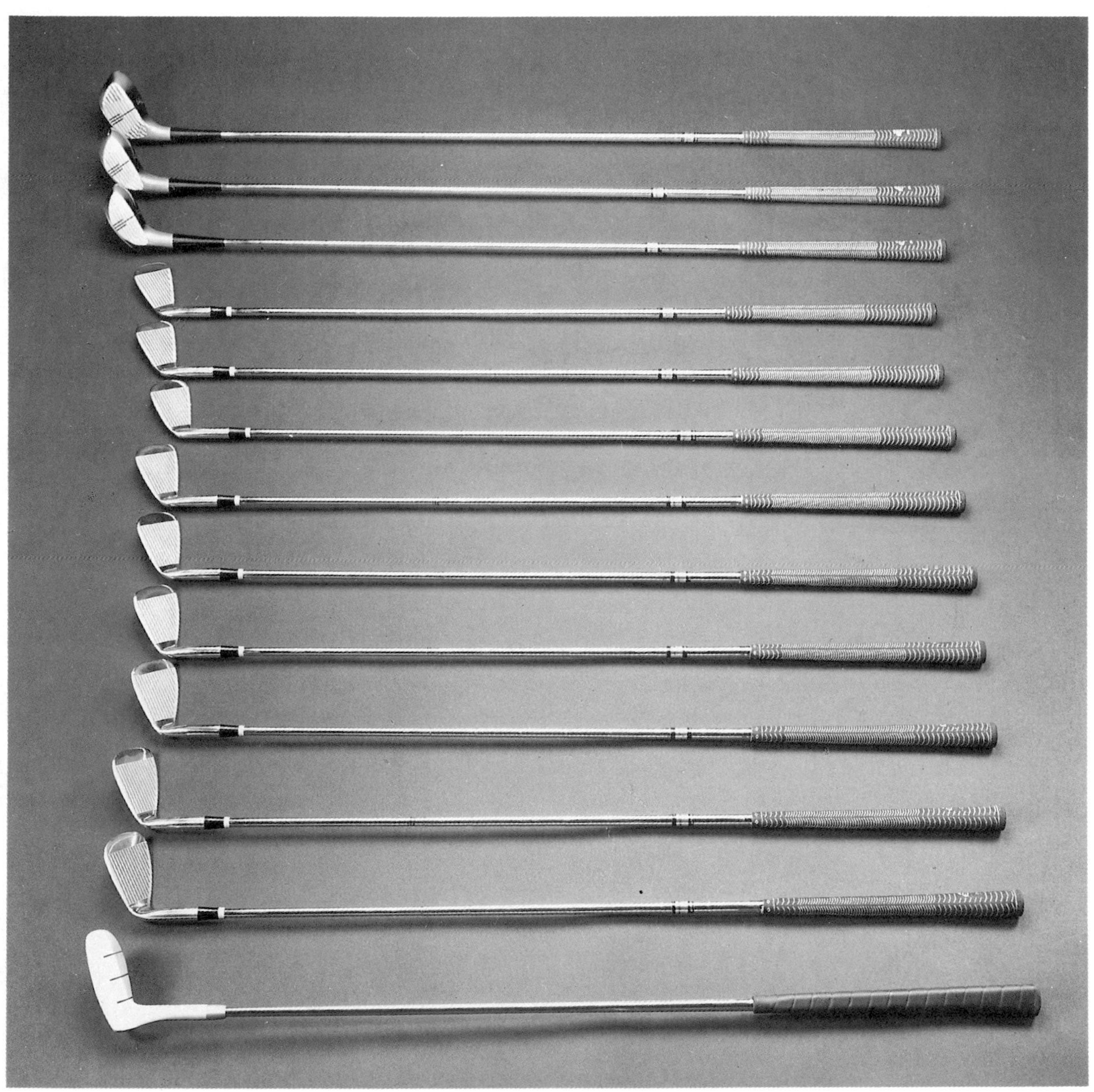

*This set of ladies' clubs (ABOVE) includes (from top to bottom) the following: driver and Nos. 3 and 5 woods; Nos. 3–9 irons; pitching wedge; sand iron; and putter. The main difference between men's and ladies' clubs is that the latter are fractionally lighter and have slightly thinner grips.*

*The set of clubs is divided into different categories, each having specific functions (RIGHT). The longest club is the driver, which is used for teeing off. This is followed by the fairway woods—here Nos. 3 and 5. The irons fall into three categories—for long-, medium- and short-range shots. Nos. 3 and 4 are long irons; Nos. 5, 6 and 7 are middle irons; and Nos. 8 and 9 are short irons. Included with the last category of irons are the pitching wedge and the sand iron, the shortest and loftiest club of all. Finally there is the putter.*

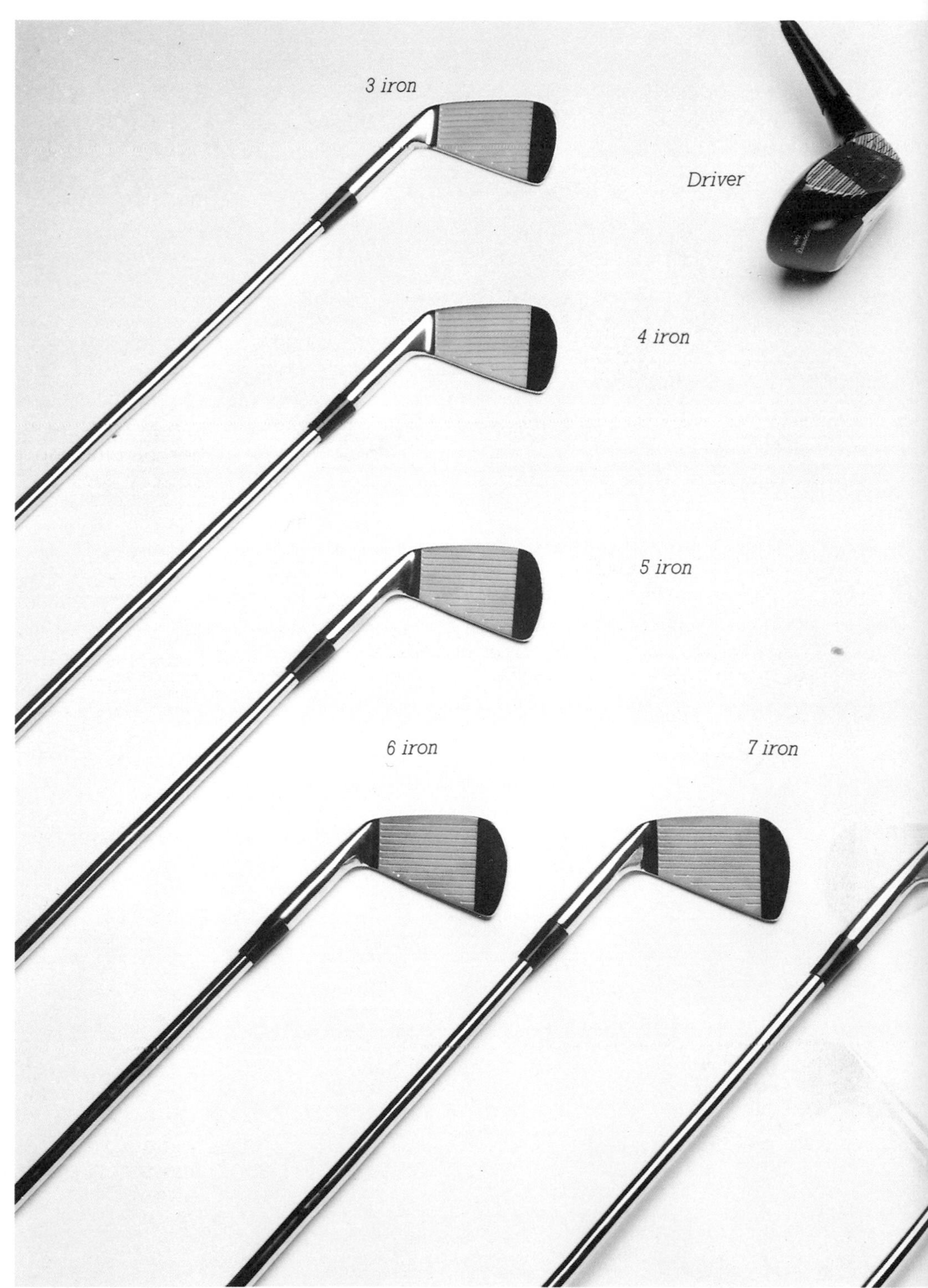

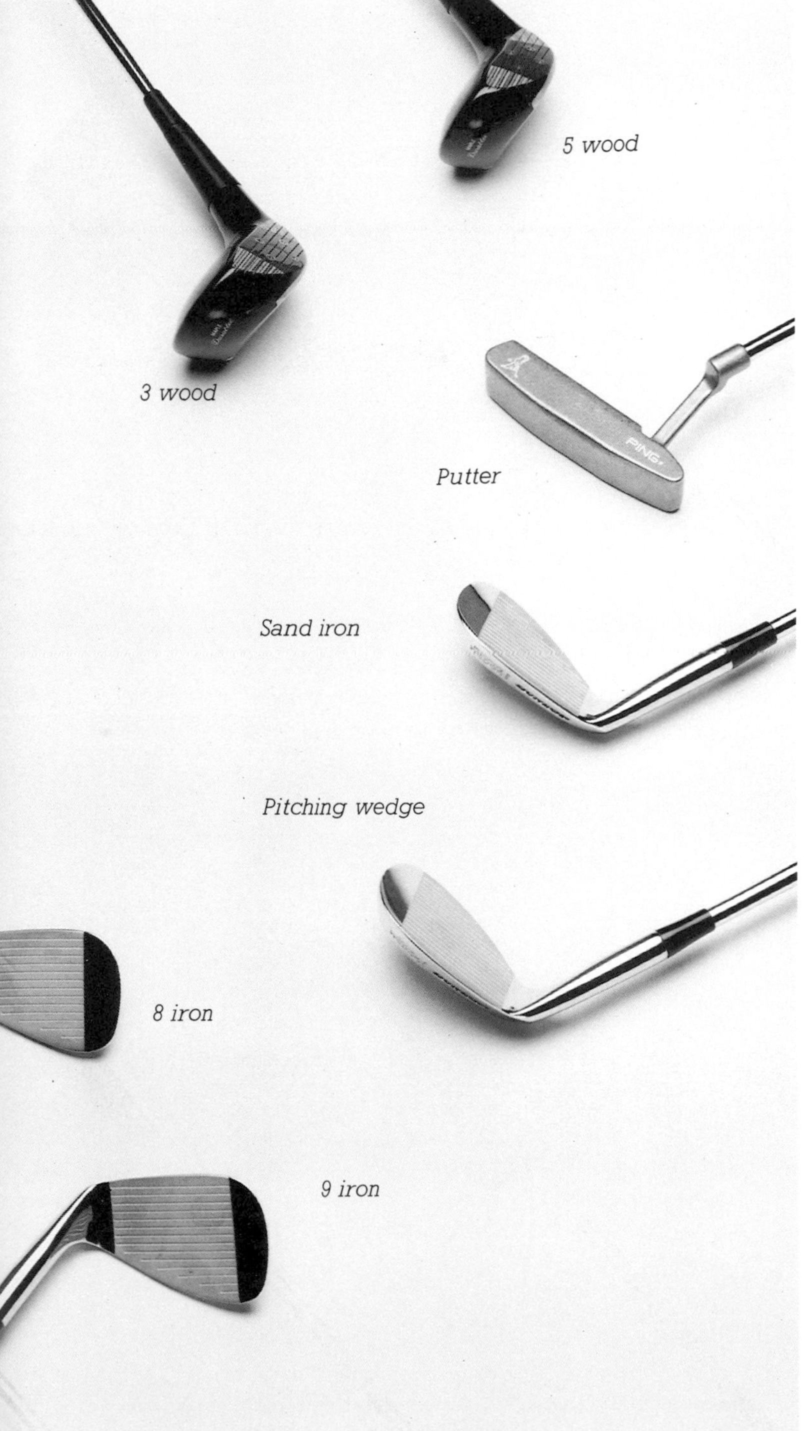


*5 wood*

*3 wood*

*Putter*

*Sand iron*

*Pitching wedge*

*8 iron*

*9 iron*

8, 9, pitching wedge and sand iron; and finally the putter.

However, until you have a reasonable feel for the sport and a pretty good idea of the type of clubs that best suit you, it is foolish to think of buying such a large set. Most beginners can quite easily manage with a half-set, which would probably be made up as follows: woods – Nos. 1 (provided it had a good amount of loft on its face) and 3; irons – either odd or even numbers (ie Nos. 3, 5, 7, and 9 or Nos. 2, 4, 6, and 8); and a putter. A sand iron is always necessary.

At the bottom end of the scale, for those with a limited budget just starting to play golf, the minimum possible number of clubs to get you going – but equally giving you a chance to make progress – is five. In this case you would need just one wood, which could be used both on the tee and the fairway. It should have a reasonable loft angle and so a No.3 would be most suitable. You will want a fair selection of irons – for long-, medium- and short-range shots. This means probably a No.3 or No.4 for long distances, a No.6 or No.7 as an intermediate iron and either a No.9 or a pitching wedge for short shots to the green and to get out of bunkers, bearing in mind these give limited results when playing from the sand. The last club would, of course, be the putter.

In principle, the idea of buying the minimum number of clubs necessary to get started and then adding as and when you can to complete the set makes a lot of sense. Unfortunately manufacturers are continually changing their ranges and you may find over a period of time that the type of clubs you bought originally are now out of stock.

It is therefore far better to buy either a half-set or the minimum amount of clubs and practice with these.

*Beginners should not buy more clubs than they need to start with. In the early stages five clubs are perfectly adequate. This selection (RIGHT)—a No.3 wood, Nos. 3, 6 and 9 irons, and a putter—would make an ideal beginner's set.*

*Molded rubber grips (BELOW) are made in two basic thicknesses. The men's grip (left) and the slightly thinner ladies' grip (right)*

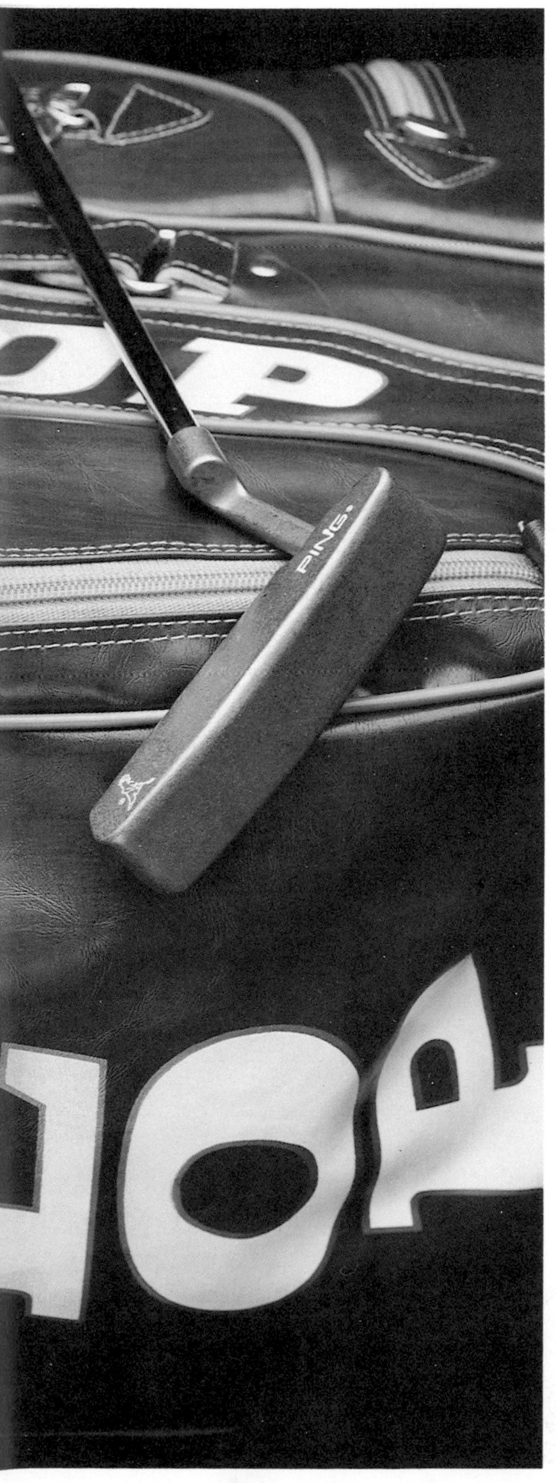


## Choosing clubs

When you do decide to buy a set of clubs, which will hopefully help you improve your game, there are many factors you must take into consideration. Having analyzed these yourself, you would be well advised to discuss your selection with a qualified professional before you actually spend any money.

**Flexibility** Clubs are available with shafts that have varying degrees of flexibility. In fact, there are five basic grades, as follows:

| | |
|---|---|
| **X-** | very stiff–for stronger professional players |
| **S-** | stiff–for the majority of professionals and other fairly strong players |
| **R-** | regular–for the majority of non-professional players |
| **A-** | weaker–for strong lady golfers and older club players |
| **L-** | weakest–for average lady golfers |

As these grades indicate, weaker players need more flexible shafts, while stronger players need stiffer shafts. When hickory was used to produce wooden shafts, these could be sand-papered down to make them thinner – and therefore more flexible. Now that steel is used to make shafts, the flexibility of the shaft is determined by the thickness of the tubing – the slimmer the tubing the more flexible the shaft.

It is possible to alter the flexibility of a club, although this is a skilled job and should be left to a professional to carry out. Shafts are designed to taper down their length toward the club-head. By taking a piece off at the bottom and adding an extension piece at the top to retain the same overall length, a thicker – and therefore stiffer – shaft can be manufactured. Conversely, by adding a piece to the handle end of the shaft, a

*As a beginner, there is no point in going to the expense of buying a full set of clubs. The wisest move, once you have established that golf really is the game for you, is to buy a half set (RIGHT). This would normally include (from left to right) the Nos.1 and 3 woods, the odd numbered irons (or the even ones), a sand iron and a putter.*

longer, more flexible club can be made. This, of course, is only practical for very tall players, since you should not play with a longer club than necessary.

**Length** Beginners often worry about the length of their clubs. However, this is not really a problem and, in fact, clubs do not vary that much at all. What is far more important is the lie of the club-head. For a tall player this needs to be more upright, while for a shorter player the lie should be much flatter (see **Lie**). Depending on the player's height, the effect the lie of the club-head has is to determine where the handle reaches in relation to the body.

Obviously for those who are particularly tall or have a short reach, the length of the club will need to vary. But as a rule, clubs should not be shortened, except if they are to be used by children. Where clubs prove to be too long in the shaft, shorter players must choose models that have a flatter lie.

You can lengthen the club by adding

on a section of dowel to the handle end. This will involve removing the grip and refitting it over the extension piece. It is not advisable, however, to extend a club shaft by more than 25mm (1in) or so, since this will put undue strain on the join when you swing the club.

Naturally, by lengthening the club you will increase its flexibility and swing weight (see **Weight**). Conversely, by shortening the shaft you will reduce the flexibility and the swing weight.

Although the length of individual clubs does vary slightly from make to make, the average length for each club is as follows:

| | | |
|---|---|---|
| **Woods-** | No.1 | 109cm (43in) |
| | No.2 | 108cm (42½in) |
| | No.3 | 107cm (42in) |
| | No.4 | 105cm (41½in) |
| | No.5 | 104cm (41in) |
| **Irons-** | No.2 | 98cm (38½in) |
| | No.3 | 97cm (38in) |
| | No.4 | 95cm (37½in) |
| | No.5 | 94cm (37in) |
| | No.6 | 93cm (36½in) |
| | No.7 | 91cm (36in) |
| | No.8 | 90cm (35½in) |
| | No.9 | 89cm (35in) |
| Pitching wedge | | 89cm (35in) |
| Sand iron | | 89cm (35in) |

**Lie** This is one of the most important aspects of a club, since with an incorrect lie you will end up adopting the wrong posture and hand position and will never develop a good and accurate swing. As will be explained later (see p. 88), most of the basic faults stem from a poor swing.

Since a beginner will always try to keep the bottom of the club-head parallel to the ground, an excessively flat or upright lie will force the player into a totally incorrect position. In extreme circumstances, for example a tall player using a club with too flat a lie, the shoulders will come over the top of the club and the hands will be forced down the handle. Equally, with a short player using a club with too steep a lie, the body will be too upright and the hands too high up on the handle.

The presence of either of these situations will have disastrous consequences for the shot. In the case of the tall player, the toe end of the club-head will dig deeper into the ground and the heel will send the ball off to the right. With the short player the reverse will happen, as the heel digs into the ground and the toe end sends the ball off to the left.

The lie of a club can be altered if, after some time, you find that it is not quite right. This is definitely not a job for the inexperienced and should be left to a professional to change.

The most important point to remember about the lie of a club is that it must be right for the individual. You should never adapt yourself, your body position or your hands to suit the club. The club must always be adapted to suit you.

**Loft** As already mentioned, golf clubs are numbered in sequence to denote the angle of loft on each of the club-faces. The angle on the face determines whether the ball, if correctly struck, flies high or low, depending on the individual shot required.

Although the angle of loft on each club-face can be varied slightly if required, normal sets of clubs do conform to a standard set of angles. These loft angles are as follows:

| | | |
|---|---|---|
| **Woods-** | No.1 | 12 degrees |
| | No.2 | 14 degrees |
| | No.3 | 16 degrees |
| | No.4 | 20 degrees |
| | No.5 | 24 degrees |
| **Irons-** | No.2 | 19 degrees |
| | No.3 | 23 degrees |
| | No.4 | 27 degrees |
| | No.5 | 31 degrees |
| | No.6 | 35 degrees |
| | No.7 | 39 degrees |
| | No.8 | 43 degrees |
| | No.9 | 47 degrees |
| Pitching wedge | | 52 degrees |
| Sand iron | | 58 degrees |

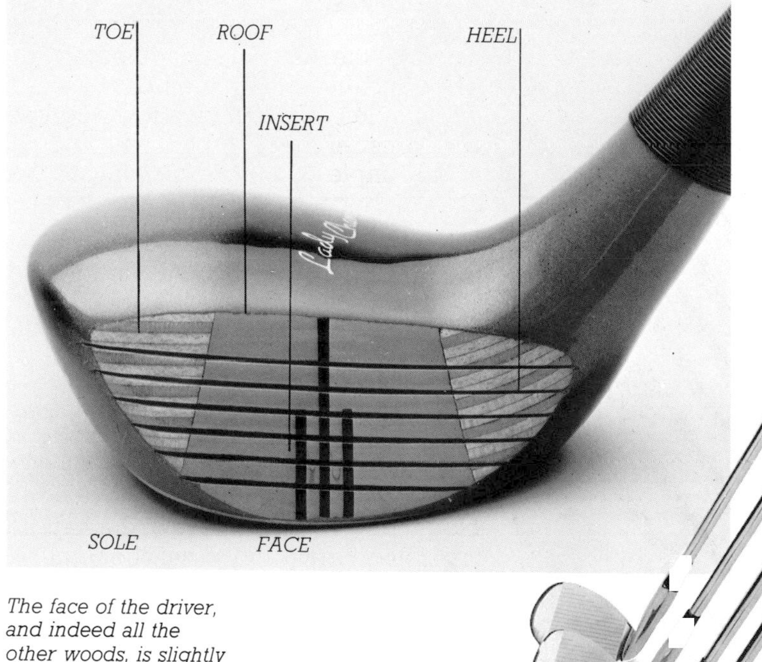


*The face of the driver, and indeed all the other woods, is slightly convex (ABOVE)—known as the "four-way roll". This delicate curve helps offer the best possible contact point when striking the ball.*

*From the set of clubs shown here (RIGHT), it is easy to see the difference in the angle of lie, from the flattest wood—the driver—right through to the steepest iron—the sand iron.*

These angles are fine for the average player. It is only the professionals who may feel the need to strengthen certain clubs and therefore sometimes have the angle of loft reduced by a few degrees where necessary.

The angle of loft on a club can be altered, but a great deal of expertise is needed to achieve a sufficiently accurate adjustment. It is particularly difficult with a wood, since the face on this type of club is slightly convex – known traditionally as the "four-way roll". Although no one has firmly established the reason for this "rounded" surface, there is no doubt that the ball flies off faster and more sweetly from it, if struck correctly.

**Thickness** The thickness of the handle of a golf club can vary to suit the requirements of the individual. Those players with smaller hands require thinner handles, while those with larger hands should have thicker ones. Because of the balance at either end of the club, one with a thinner handle will make the clubhead feel heavier, while one with a thicker handle will make it feel lighter. In either case, you may well decide you need to alter the overall weight of the club to maintain the correct balance, which is vital for successful swinging (see **Weight**).

It should be remembered that the thicker the handle, the less you will feel the action of your hands. Conversely, the thinner the handle the more you will feel the action of your hands.

The simplest way to alter the thickness of the handle is to change the grip. There are basically two types of grip – one for men and one for ladies. Should the change of grip not be sufficient, it is possible to pack out the handle under the grip by binding on extra tape before fitting it.

**Weight** This refers to two aspects of the club – the actual *overall weight* and the *swing weight*. It is important that the swing weight suits the individual needs of each player. Although the variations are very slight, alterations can be made quite easily.

To ensure accurate and consistent swinging throughout the range of clubs, it is vital that each club has a similar feel to it when you swing back and then down into the shot. This means that to keep the swing weight relatively constant, the overall weight of individual clubs has to be different. That is why clubs with longer shafts are lighter than those with shorter shafts. However, there is still plenty of choice available since, although manufacturers do maintain fairly constant swing weights in clubs, the actual overall weights do vary from make to make. Here, however, are the average weights of the various clubs:

| | | |
|---|---|---|
| **Woods-** | No.1 | 376g (13¼oz) |
| | No.2 | 383g (13½oz) |
| | No.3 | 390g (13¾oz) |
| | No.4 | 397g (14oz) |
| | No.5 | 404g (14¼oz) |
| **Irons-** | No.2 | 397g (14oz) |
| | No.3 | 404g (14¼oz) |
| | No.4 | 411g (14½oz) |
| | No.5 | 418g (14¾oz) |
| | No.6 | 425g (15oz) |
| | No.7 | 432g (15¼oz) |
| | No.8 | 439g (15½oz) |
| | No.9 | 446g (15¾oz) |
| Pitching wedge | | 454g (16oz) |
| Sand iron | | 461g (16¼oz) |

On average, ladies' clubs are fractionally lighter, although rarely by more than an ounce.

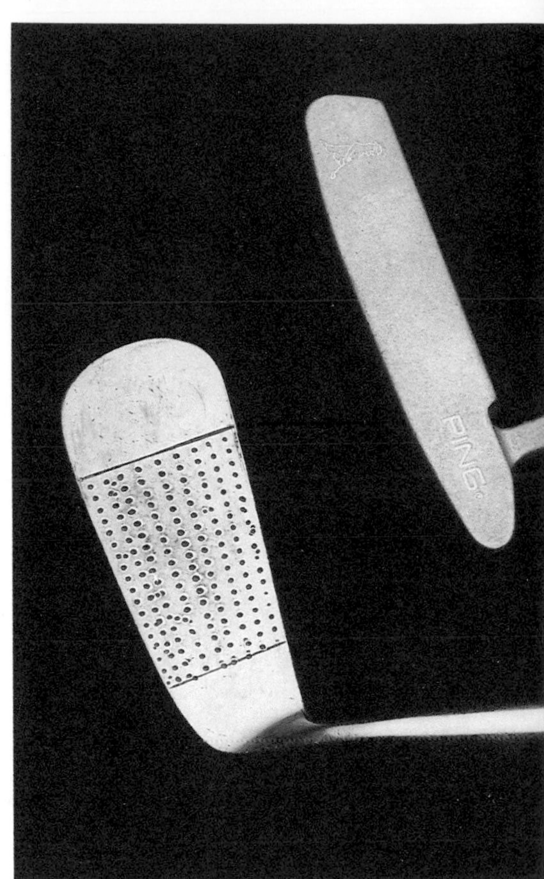

## Choosing a putter

There is a wide range of putters currently available, and you will only be in a position to select the one that suits you best once you have mastered the technique for striking the ball on the green. Putting is a critical part of the game of golf and it is therefore very important to use a putter that has, for you, the correct balance and feel.

Unfortunately more putters get discarded than any other club in the set, since this is the area where golfers generally suffer the most problems. More often than not the putter will be made the scapegoat as players strive to improve their techniques on the greens. You will, in fact, find that in many professional shops there is a ready supply of excellent second-hand putters, for these are regularly traded in by frus-

*The putter tends to create more problems than any other club—and it is the one that gets discarded most quickly. Throughout the history of the game, manufacturers have tried to produce the ideal putter, some examples of which are shown here (RIGHT). These include (from top to bottom) the "Ray Cook" putter; the Ping; the light-bladed "Acushnet"; the 1928 traditional "Staynorus" version; and the standard design putter.*

*The design of putters has changed enormously over the years, as you can see from this contrast between a modern Ping putter and the traditional hickory-shafted one (LEFT); this example dates from 1928. Deciding which putter is the best for you is largely a matter of trial and error.*

trated golfers.

There are no hard and fast rules about which putter to choose. As a general guide, however, most of the branded models should prove adequate until you decide you need a change or the improvement in your technique demands one. For older players, ladies and youngsters, the putter should be on the shorter, light side.

## Club maintenance

However well you manage to develop and improve your game, consistently successful golf will to a certain extent depend on the quality and condition of your clubs. For the sake of your own performance and also to avoid unnecessary expenditure, you must look after your clubs properly.

In the course of a round of golf – or

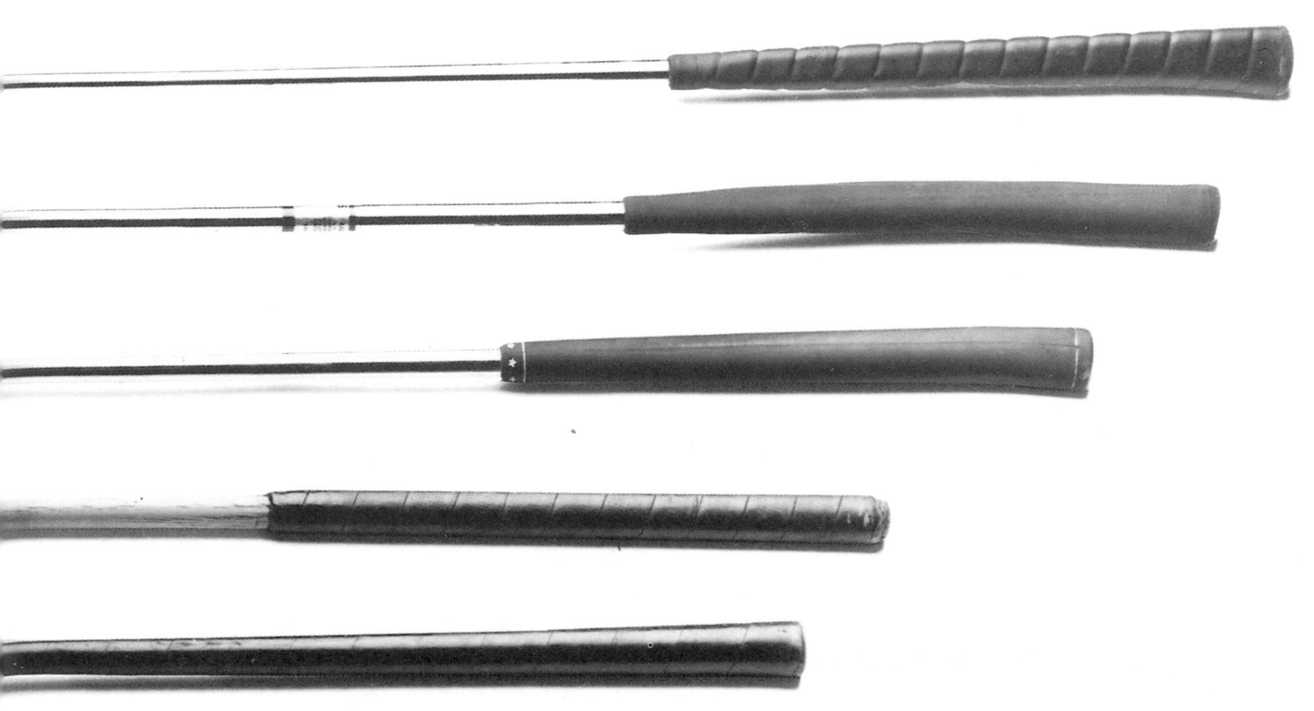

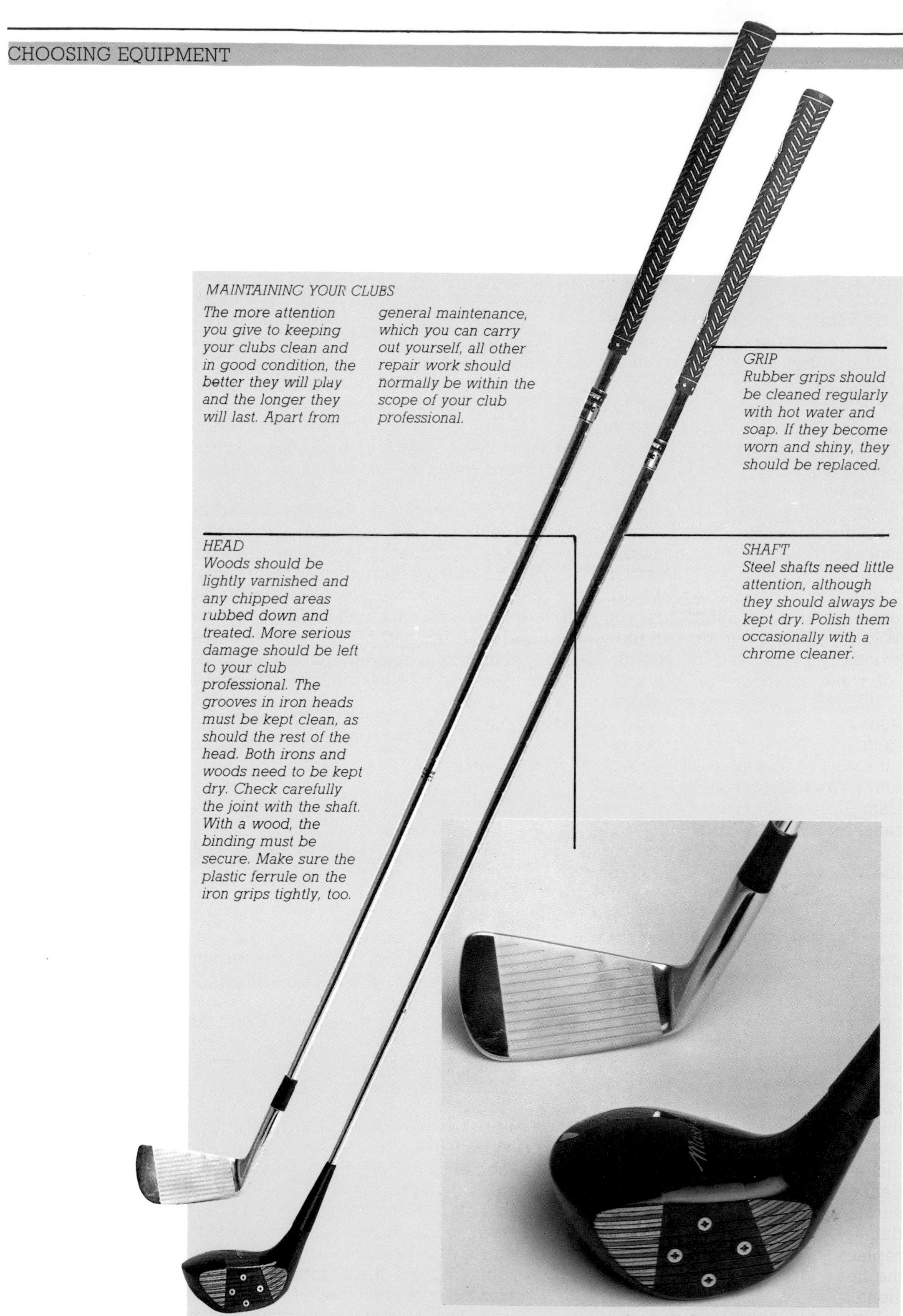

*MAINTAINING YOUR CLUBS*

*The more attention you give to keeping your clubs clean and in good condition, the better they will play and the longer they will last. Apart from general maintenance, which you can carry out yourself, all other repair work should normally be within the scope of your club professional.*

*GRIP*

*Rubber grips should be cleaned regularly with hot water and soap. If they become worn and shiny, they should be replaced.*

*HEAD*

*Woods should be lightly varnished and any chipped areas rubbed down and treated. More serious damage should be left to your club professional. The grooves in iron heads must be kept clean, as should the rest of the head. Both irons and woods need to be kept dry. Check carefully the joint with the shaft. With a wood, the binding must be secure. Make sure the plastic ferrule on the iron grips tightly, too.*

*SHAFT*

*Steel shafts need little attention, although they should always be kept dry. Polish them occasionally with a chrome cleaner.*

even during practice – your clubs are bound to pick up some dirt. It is very important that you clean them after each shot *and* certainly when you have finished with them at the end of the day. The grooves on the club-face of your irons must be kept free of dirt to insure the best possible contact with the ball, particularly when you want to effect back spin.

If the clubs get wet, always wipe them down and dry them thoroughly at the end of your round. They should then be stored in a room with a stable temperature. Do not be tempted to put them near a fire or other form of direct heat to dry out – let them dry naturally. If you store your clubs without drying them, the woods will swell and in extreme cases rot, while the irons will go rusty.

It is important to remember that if you use headcovers – which you should certainly do on woods to prevent the clubs being damaged as they are put in and pulled out of the bag – never leave damp heads in covers when you have finished playing.

Woods need particular attention to the insert in the club-face, where contact is – or should be – made with the ball. Since the wood around the insert has to put up with a lot of harsh treatment, the varnish tends to chip. If dirt and moisture settle in these chipped areas, the wood soon gets softer and rapidly deteriorates.

You should also make sure that the binding around the neck is always secure and check that the joint between the neck and the shaft is sound. If you let this work loose, the neck will split.

Always keep your woods lightly varnished. If you do detect any signs of damage, rub the wood down to a sound surface and then revarnish the damaged area. All other repairs, such as replacing the insert and repositioning the head, should be left to the professional.

With irons, apart from keeping them clean and dry, you should also check the area where the shaft enters the head. If water gets in under the plastic ferrule, this part of the shaft will, after a time, start to rust and consequently weaken the club. Should a gap appear between the ferrule and the head, try holding the ferrule under a very hot faucet. You should then be able to move it down easily to seal the gap.

As well as looking after the club-head, you must also make sure that no moisture is left on the chromium-plated shafts. Otherwise tiny spots of rust will start to appear and these could quickly spread. Provided you keep the shafts dry, no other maintenance should be required except, perhaps, a periodical polish with a suitable chrome cleaner.

The grip, traditionally made of leather but now almost exclusively of rubber, should be cleaned once a month with hot water and soap. A good scrub should be enough to take off the shine. However, a grip that has become excessively worn and shiny should be replaced before it starts to have an adverse effect on your handling.

## The balls

The golf ball has had a varied history, and the types currently available have developed through many different stages over the years. The size of the ball is soon to be standardized at 4.3cm (1.68in) in diameter – as opposed to the 4.1cm(1.62in) original – although the existing standard weight of 46g (1.62oz) will be maintained.

There will, however, still be a choice as to the ball's compression, which is determined by the tension of the rubber strands that are wound around the core before the ball is covered. The standard ball has a 90 compression, while the harder model has a 100 compression. Naturally the harder ball, given the right conditions, will travel further than the lower compression ball if struck correctly. This advantage is minimized in

*It is not only the composition but also the type of surface that gives a golf ball specific characteristics in flight. The number and depth of dimples is significant. The deeper the dimples, the more the ball will lift. Of the three balls shown here (BELOW), the one in the center is the most revolutionary. It has been designed as a dodecahedron, with 12 identical sides. With this ball it is possible to trace 10 equators without touching a dimple.*

cold weather since the rubber does not warm up, and even the longer hitting players should revert to the 90 compression ball in these circumstances. For the average golfer, the lower compression ball is recommended.

You may, of course, decide to try to gain extra length by using a harder ball. However, this should only be attempted when you can guarantee a high degree of accuracy in the shot. Remember that you will inevitably have to sacrifice a little with the shorter, more delicate shots since you cannot change your ball during the playing of a specific hole. Depending on the rules of the country you are playing in, you may even have to retain one type of ball throughout the whole round.

The composition of the golf ball has undergone several changes in recent years. As well as the traditional ball, with rubber strands wound around a solid inner core, there are now balls with a larger solid center and less rubber and even some that are completely solid. While the harder balls will travel further, they are not particularly suitable for short shots, such as pitching to the green, since you cannot impart as much back spin on them as you can on wound balls. Likewise you will not get as good a feel from them when playing gentle shots, especially when putting.

The composition of the inside of the ball is not the only factor that affects the way it plays. The dimpling on the outside is also instrumental. Although the

actual shape of the dimples has been altered many times without any significant difference, it is certainly true that a ball with shallow dimples will not lift significantly, while one with deep dimples may well lift too much. There is even a ball being produced which flies shorter distances for use on courses built in restricted areas. At the same time it is supposed to give a similar impression as the normal ball on longer courses. But that is for the future!

At the end of the day, only practice will determine the most suitable type of golf ball for your particular game. Your selection, therefore, must be based on trial and error – and, to a lesser degree, on the prevailing conditions on the course.

*Golf balls have changed a lot over the years, the earliest versions being almost unrecognizable alongside the modern types. Shown here (BELOW) are three of the oldest styles— (from left to right) the feathery, the bramble pattern and the chisel-marked gutty.*

*The compression of a golf ball is important. In this technological age, there are even machines to test the degree of compression (INSET) and the durability of the casing (LEFT).*

## The dress

Whatever you wear when practicing or playing golf, it is essential that the various items of clothing are both comfortable and practical. There are no hard and fast rules about the exact clothing that can be worn on the course, although the majority of established clubs have fairly strict standards and these must be adhered to if you are visiting one. It is essential to wear clothing that permits free movement and there is an excellent selection of golfing shirts and sweaters, as well as slacks to choose from.

It is worth remembering that you may be out on the course for several hours at a time, so be prepared for any dramatic changes in the weather. It is often worth taking an extra sweater with you in case you start to feel the cold. It is an obvious point, but one worth repeating, that cold limbs and joints are one of a player's worst enemies.

**Waterproof suit** Prolonged heavy rain will eventually curtail your practice or round of golf. You will probably try to play through the odd shower and, in competitions, may well have to until the course is pronounced unplayable, so a waterproof suit is a wise investment.

Traditionally these suits were made of cotton, but they suffered from being a bit on the heavy side and tended to restrict the wearer's golfing action. For this reason people often used to wear the waterproof trousers by themselves. More recent designs now make use of lightweight plastic materials. This type of waterproof suit is much easier to play in since it does not absorb any moisture and thus does not restrict movement. An added benefit is its compactness, which means it can be wrapped up into a small package and easily fit into a golf bag.

It is worth bearing in mind that a waterproof suit is not only useful for protecting you from the rain. It can also offer protection when you have to play a ball from a particularly awkward lie, such as in a thorny bush or shrub.

**Golf shoes** To insure a sound footing on the ground when playing a stroke – which is essential for accurate and powerful swinging – you must wear suitable golf shoes. Today there is a basic choice between metal spikes and rubber studs.

Ground conditions will to a large degree determine which is best. In muddy and slippery grass metal spikes are definitely preferable to rubber studs, since they will enable you to

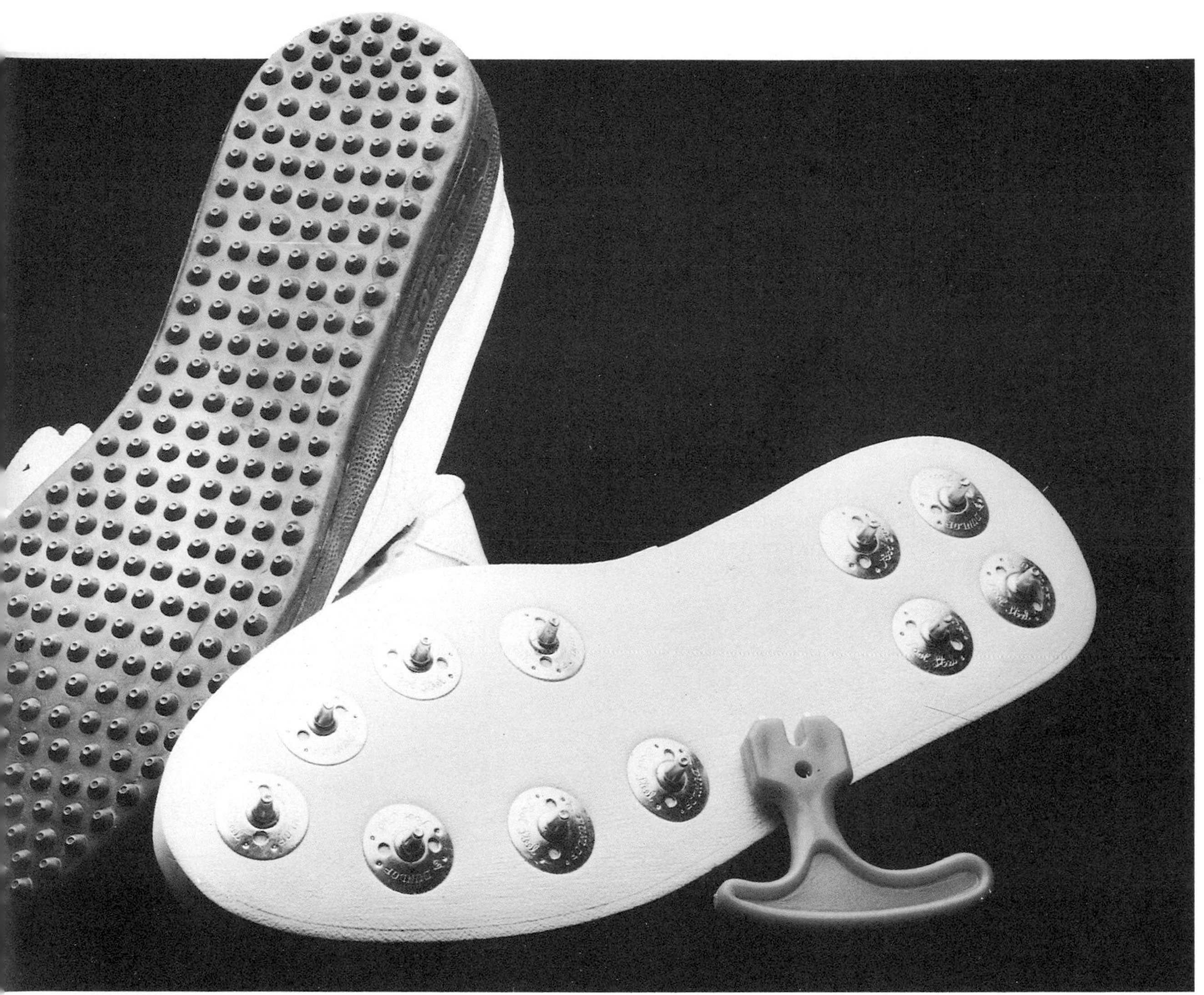

achieve a much firmer grip with your feet. In normal conditions, however, rubber-studded shoes have proved increasingly popular in recent years.

**Golf glove** A glove is not an essential part of a golfer's dress, although the vast majority of players do wear one. There is little doubt that a good quality glove will help maximize the grip on the club-handle. Incidentally, for a right-handed player the glove is always worn on the left hand – and vice-versa for a left-handed player.

As with most items of dress and equipment, there is a wide price and quality range. Although it is not necessary to buy the best, a good quality glove will last twice as long as a cheap one.

You should always try to keep the glove slightly moist and supple. It is advisable to rub cream over the glove every so often to prevent it from going hard and cracking. You will find it difficult to maintain a glove that is perpetually saturated in heavy rain. In these conditions it is wise to have an old glove handy to take the worst of the rain.

*Footwear is a crucial part of a golfer's dress (ABOVE), since a firm footing is all-important for accurate, powerful swinging. Although rubber-soled shoes are adequate in drier conditions, spiked ones are definitely preferable when the ground is wet and slippery. The spiked studs can be unscrewed with a special key and replaced.*

*Apart from the wide range of clothes available to suit all tastes, including colorful shirts and sweaters (MAIN PICTURE), a waterproof suit such as this one being worn by the 1985 British Open champion Sandy Lyle (INSET) is an indispensable item of clothing.*

5
DUNLOP
65i
M
Slazenger

*When choosing a golf bag (RIGHT) it is important to make sure that it is large enough to take all your clubs and the many extras that you may wish to carry around with you. Forcing clubs into a tight and crowded bag will take a heavy toll on the shafts and grips. A trolley—which should have suitably wide wheels—will, of course, ease the strain on your shoulder.*

*For those occasions when you are playing with a half-set and are not carrying many extras, the small "Sunday bag" is the most suitable.*

## The extras

As with any other sport – and probably more so than some – golf has attracted many items of paraphernalia that have little to do with how well equipped you are or how well you play. Do not be tempted to be seen to be playing the part by cluttering up your golf bag with unnecessary bits and pieces. Not only will these make your load a lot heavier and therefore tire you out more quickly as you tote them all around the course, but they are just as likely to distract you from the job in hand – and that is playing the best golf you can.

**Golf bag** This, of course, is an essential item, since you will not only want something to carry your set of clubs around in, but you also need it to take your golf balls, tee pegs, a cloth to wipe your clubs, probably a towel and cap (in very sunny weather) and possibly a waterproof suit as well.

It is important to remember that your golf bag must be large enough for you to pull out and slide back your clubs easily and freely. A lot of damage can be done by trying to force a club back into a bag that is already jammed full – the grips, in particular, will wear down that much quicker. Bearing in mind the weight you will be carrying around on your shoulder for hours at a time, you should make sure that the strap is wide and well-padded. If not, it will soon start cutting into your shoulder and will make life quite unbearable.

There is a smaller version of the standard golf bag known as the "Sunday bag." It is quite useful for those occasions when you are only playing with a half-set of clubs and not carrying around a lot of extra items.

**Golf trolley** Provided you get a good sturdy model with wide wheels that is not too heavy to pull around, a trolley can be a very worthwhile investment particularly if you play a lot of golf on hilly

*There is always plenty of paraphernalia to tempt the impressionable amateur golfer. However, you will soon discover that it is unwise to burden yourself more than is necessary, and so you should only carry those items of equipment that are absolutely essential (OVERLEAF). These include a golf glove to insure a positive grip; a sun visor in good weather and an umbrella for bad; a towel on which to wipe the ball and clubs; and headcovers to protect the clubs from the rain. The final choice is a personal one, but remember not to overload yourself—you need all your strength to play the round.*

DUNLOP

Maxfli
Maxfli
DDH

courses. It is certainly advisable for the less strong or older players who want to reserve their energy for playing shots. If you do buy a trolley, make sure that your golf bag has an internal frame to prevent it collapsing when fitted to the trolley.

A further point to bear in mind when choosing a trolley is the width of the wheels, especially if you intend to carry relatively heavy loads in your bag. You will very quickly be pulled up and admonished if your progress around the course is being marked by a deep set of wheel ruts!

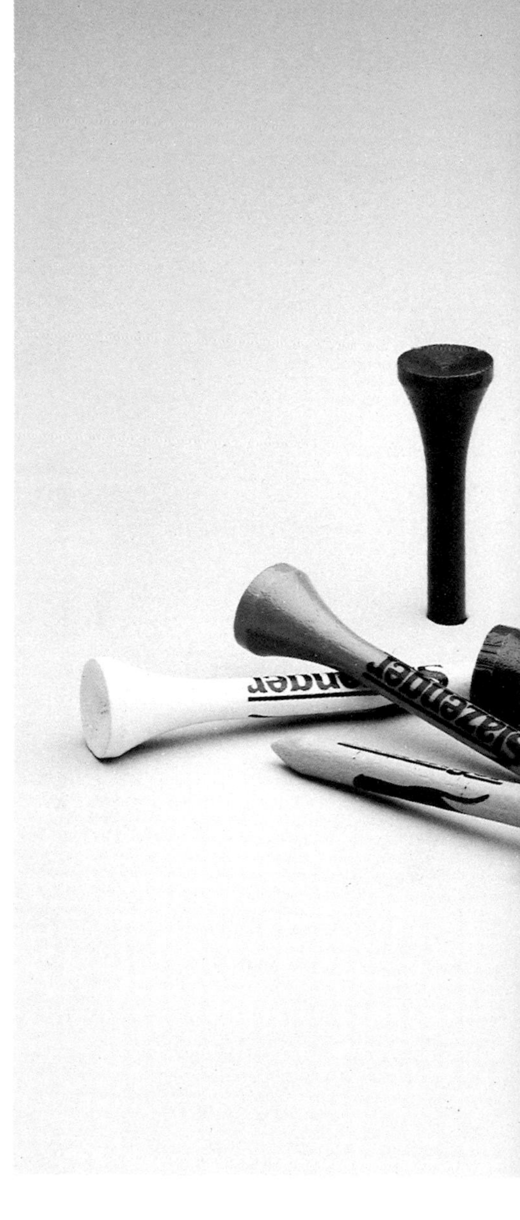

**Tee pegs** Having flirted briefly with rubber, manufacturers have now settled for either wooden or plastic tee pegs. Many players prefer wooden pegs since they do not mark the face of the woods. You will need to carry around a supply of pegs since they do have a knack of disappearing when you have played your tee shot. As a point of etiquette, you should always make a habit of picking up your tee peg after the shot – even if the pegs are provided free at the start of each hole, as they often are at some of the more expensive golf clubs. Many of these clubs are, however, withdrawing this generosity since abandoned pegs are causing considerable damage to the grass-cutting machines.

**Ball marker and pitchfork** These are two essential items for use on the putting greens. The marker is a disk, usually made of plastic, which you place directly behind the ball when you need to lift it, either for cleaning or to get it out of the line of another player's shot.

The pitchfork should be used very carefully to repair the pitchmark caused by a ball landing with force on a green. The fork is used to gently raise the impacted area which is then tapped smooth with the bottom of the putter.

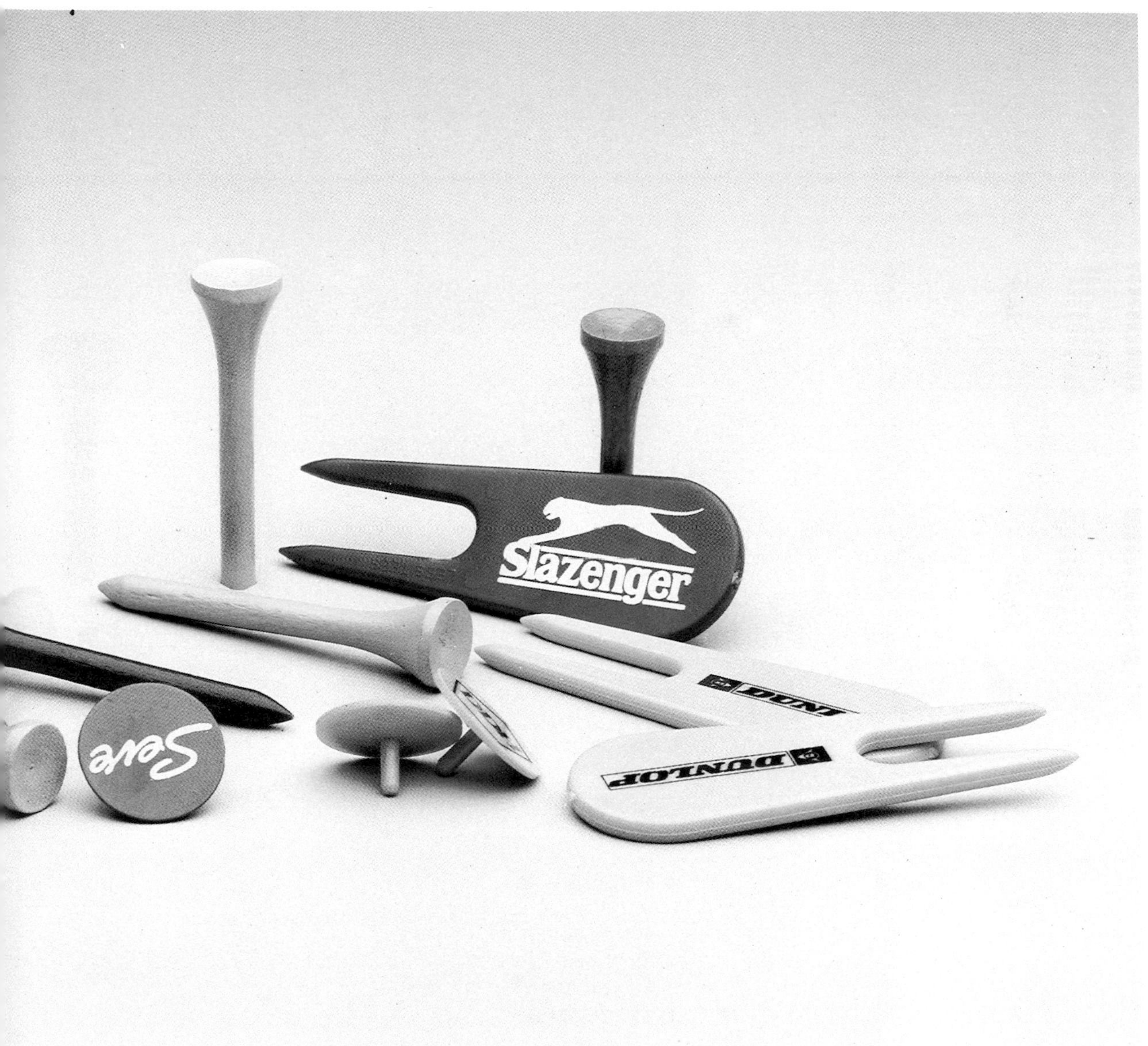


*The choice of tee peg (ABOVE) is between wooden and plastic, with many golfers preferring the former to prevent the face of the woods being marked. Essential items when you reach the putting greens are a ball marker and a small pitchfork to repair any marks your ball makes when landing on the green.*

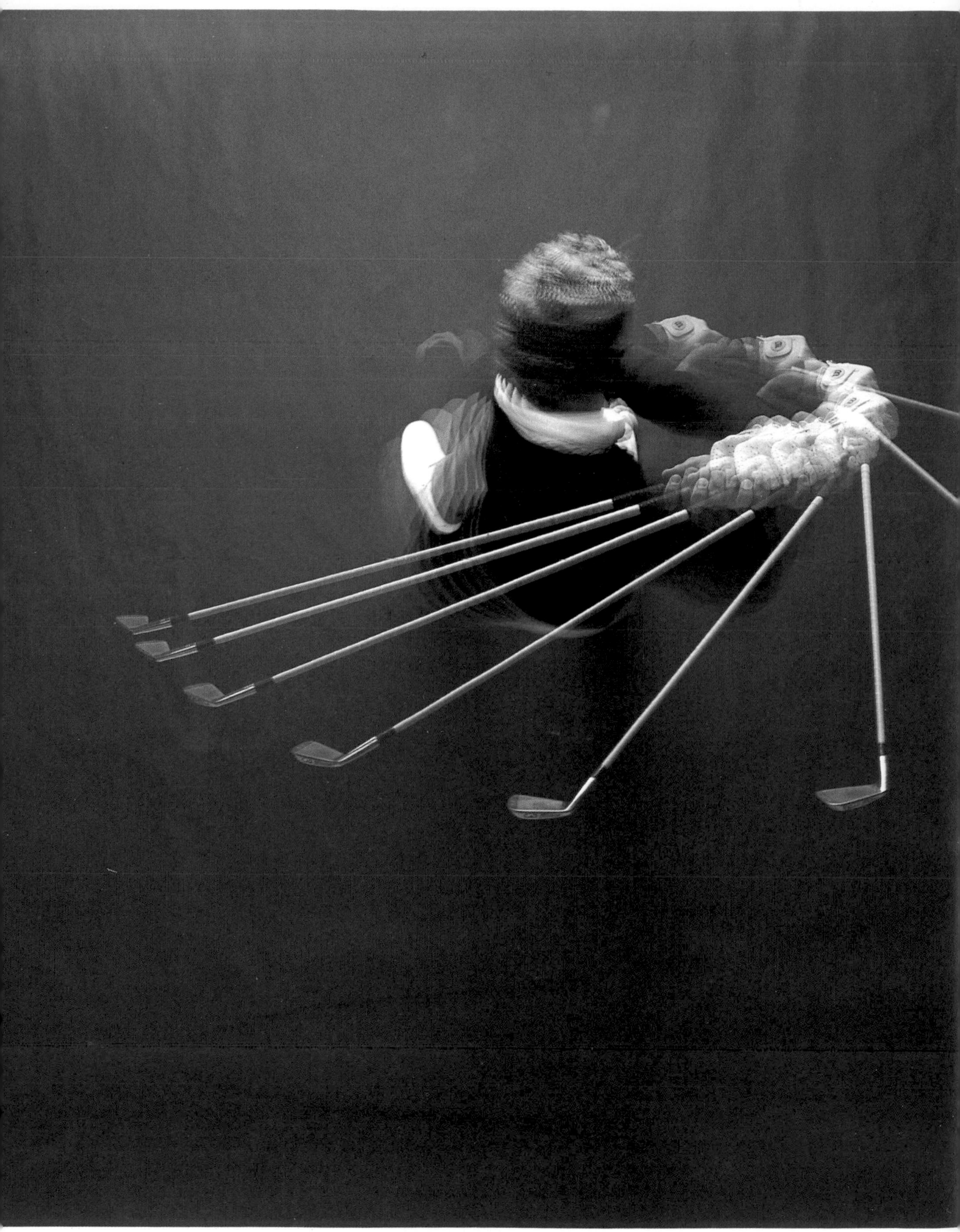

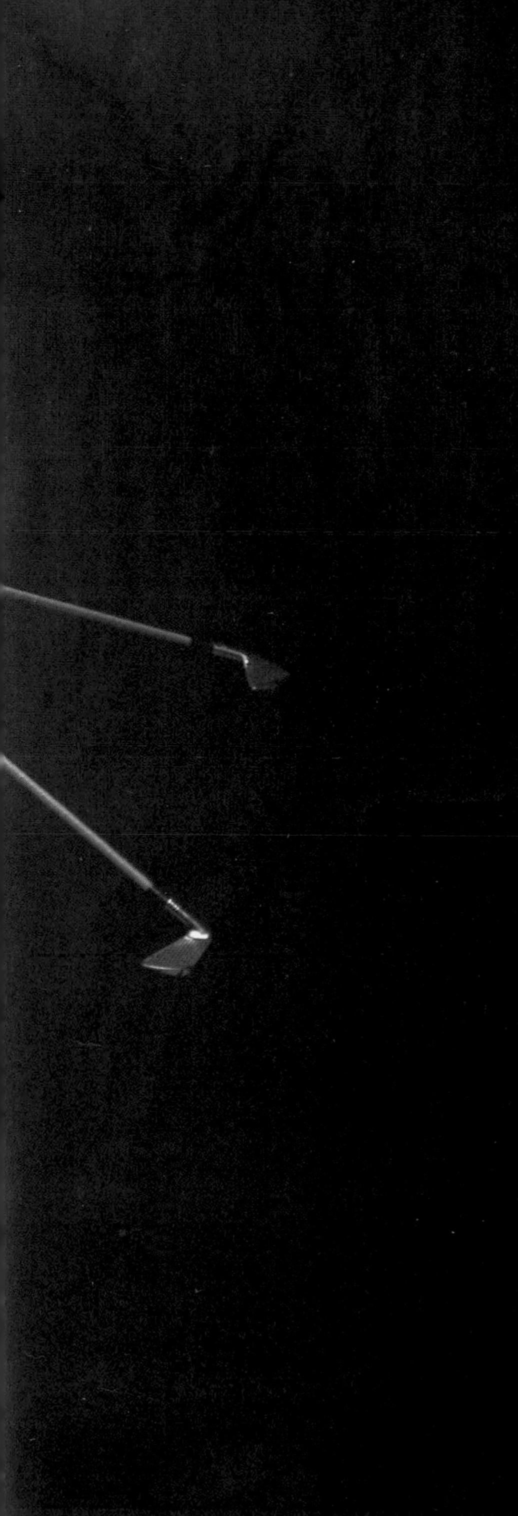

SECTION TWO

# LEARNING THE BASICS

The key to a successful golfing technique is a thorough understanding of the three basic elements involved – the stance, the grip and the swing. No matter how hard you try to put together the rest of your game, you are bound to meet with failure if you cannot go through these elementary routines correctly and consistently.

Each of these basics is dealt with here separately and described in detail and in the order of application. They may appear to make you feel disjointed and the individual sequences artificial as you learn them, but it takes only a short time for the setting-up process to become a smooth ritual.

There is no point in rushing through this section of the book in order to get to the more unusual shots or the methods for solving problems and getting out of trouble. The more time you spend practicing and perfecting the basics, the better equipped you will be to tackle the more sophisticated and demanding aspects of golf. Even if you have been playing the game for some time, it always pays to stand back and look at the elementary principles again. The chances are that any faults you have developed can be corrected, although this may mean starting again from scratch.

Settling into the correct stance should always be your first consideration – even before you take up your grip on the club. There are important reasons for this, which will be made clear later. However, what you must always keep in mind is that the stance dictates other crucial aspects of the shot, such as the direction of the swing and that in which the ball travels.

*Establishing the correct ball-to-target line (ABOVE LEFT) is the vital first step when setting up for the shot. When you are satisfied you have selected the correct line, you must then aim the club along that imaginary line (ABOVE).*

## Setting up for the shot

Many of the faults that can occur in the swing result from an incorrect or poor execution of the setting-up procedure. The first step in this procedure is to establish the aim for the shot by lining up the club and the ball with the target.

To begin, you must stand square to the ball, although slightly further away than would be necessary for the shot, leaning over it and looking up and down the imaginary line from the ball to the target. Then take the club you have chosen for the shot in your right hand, reach forward and position it with the face of the club against the ball and square to the target line.

The next move is to bring your right foot forward into position. Where you place it is all-important to the effectiveness and accuracy of the swing, since it will determine the eventual position of the legs and hips when you make contact with the ball.

Having established the best position for the right foot, bring your left foot up into line with the right, parallel to the imaginary target line, and pass the club from the right hand into the left one. This will cause your left shoulder to come forward into position to help control the swing. Then, once you have settled yourself into a comfortable position, you can return your right hand onto the club-handle.

*The final part of establishing the correct aim is to bring the left foot up in line with the right so that both are parallel to the imaginary ball-to-target line (FAR LEFT). To insure the shoulders adopt the right line, the club should be passed from the right hand into the left (BOTTOM LEFT). The final movement before entering the swing sequence is to put the right hand back on the club-handle (LEFT).*

Depending on the type of club being used and the shot you intend to play, you should lean your body forward slightly from the waist and slightly sideways to the left into the shot. This is more necessary with the shorter clubs than the long ones, and you will find that a slight inward flexing of the right knee helps. The base of the club-head should be just resting on the ground and maintained true to the target. This posture determines the eventual angle at which you will swing the club around your body – commonly known as the *swing plane.*

It is vital at this stage that you should feel totally comfortable, so it is advisable, when learning, to use a club of manageable length and loft, say a No. 6

*In the set-up routine there are three basic stances that can be adopted — square, open and closed. With a square stance (ABOVE) the shoulders, hips and feet are all parallel to the imaginary ball-to-target line. With an open stance (ABOVE RIGHT) the shoulders, hips and feet aim to the left of this line, while with a closed stance (RIGHT) these all point to the right of the imaginary line. Many professionals practice their stance by using a club on the ground aimed directly at the target, which allows them to check their accuracy.*

iron. (A long wood can ruin early control, while a short lofted iron allows too many errors to go unnoticed.) Your weight distribution, although forward, should be evenly balanced, allowing you perfect mobility. To test this, you should now move the club away from and to the ball a few times. Not only will this determine the shape of your swing, but it will also help you to keep your hands, wrists and arms supple. With the longer clubs, you will need to move your knees and shoulders as well when going through this simple exercise.

You must position the club-face square to the ball along the line of the intended shot *before* you take up the necessary stance, rather than take up the stance you believe to be the correct one and *then* adjust the angle of the club-face. How accurately you place the club-head against the ball will determine the accuracy of the final direction of the shot.

## Taking up the stance

There are several basic factors that determine the correct stance. First you must establish the distance your feet should be from the ball. This will depend on the length of the club you have chosen for the shot, which will also determine the width of the stance – that is, how far apart your feet are. You should work this out by practicing with each of the clubs in your set. In this way you should know as soon as you select a club what distance away from the ball

*The perfect set-up position for the drive (FAR LEFT). Although the ball is well forward in the stance, it has not influenced the shoulder line, which remains parallel to the imaginary ball-to-target line. With a closed stance (LEFT) you can see clearly how the line of the shoulders is influenced in relation to the target.*

*There are basically two methods of taking up the stance and insuring the ball is positioned correctly in relation to the feet. Less experienced golfers—particularly those with high handicaps — should adopt the technique whereby the ball is played opposite the inside of the left foot with the driver (ABOVE) and is moved back gradually to a central position in the stance as you work through the irons in the set (ABOVE RIGHT).*

you should stand and how far apart your feet should be.

Another important factor to consider is the position of your feet in relation to the ball – and here there are two methods you may choose from. You will be relieved to learn, however, that both have the same effect on the width of your stance, which changes depending on the club you use, regardless of the choice of method.

The width of your stance will, as already mentioned, depend on the type of club you are using. When playing with a wood, your feet should be as far apart as your normal walking stride. Shorten this width slightly when using the longer irons (ie. No. 3 or No. 4). With the shorter irons, the width of your stance should be just over half that of your stance for the woods.

One method, and that favored by most professionals, is to have the inside of the left foot opposite the ball for all shots. As the length of the club being used becomes shorter, the width of the stance is narrowed by bringing the right foot closer to the left. Of course the stance becomes closer to the ball, accordingly. While this would appear to be the easier method, it is the most dangerous for the learner, since there is a great urge to turn the shoulders away from being parallel to the target line when the shorter irons are being used.

The other method, which is strongly recommended for all learners, involves taking up the stance where the ball is played from, opposite the left heel, and varying it to directly between the feet, according to the club. With a wood, the ball should be positioned well forward in the stance, whereas with the shorter irons it should be more central.

The general principle is that for a normal shot the ball should be at the bottom of the swing as you bring the club-head down and into the strike. With the shor-

ter irons, when you need a downward contact on the ball and one which imparts more back spin, the ball should be positioned further back in the stance. On the other hand, with a wood you should make a sweeping contact on the ball and therefore have it positioned further forward in the stance. It has been suggested that a driver actually catches the ball on its upswing from the base of the arc and the ball may, therefore, be positioned well forward.

Naturally the actual position of the ball in relation to the feet will be determined through practice. However, it is more rewarding for beginners to start by adopting different stances and then, as your ability grows, to decide whether the advantages of a single ball position make it worth changing to, bearing in mind that many experts prefer not to risk damaging their shoulder line, which they consider more important.

As for the direction, ideally you should try to develop your stance so that your left foot aligns with your right foot in a line parallel to the target line. Beginners have a tendency to leave their left foot slightly behind their right, which results in a fractionally open stance. This does, in fact, assist in developing a good swing and is far less serious a problem than bringing your left foot in front of the right. This is known as a closed stance. It is very difficult to develop a good through swing in this position since it causes poor use of your hands and shoulders in turning the face of the club round as a means of sending the ball toward the target.

Your shoulders are also very much part of the set-up procedure, since the line they adopt will determine the line through which you swing your club. For normal shots, where your stance is square on, the line of your shoulders should be parallel to the line of the shot. Within this lining-up, the actual level of

*Many professional golfers prefer to play the ball in a constant forward position regardless of the length of the club (ABOVE LEFT). Although this method — which involves bringing the right foot gradually closer to the left (ABOVE) to narrow the stance — may sound simpler, it is only advisable and suitable when you can guarantee complete swing control.*

each shoulder will depend on the type of club being used. The longer the club, the higher the left shoulder will be than the right. Taking the other extreme, with the shortest clubs the left shoulder will be only slightly higher than the right.

Having found the right line for the shoulders – depending on the shot being played – as well as the level, you must establish the correct angle through which to swing the club. This is achieved by bending your spine slightly forward and bringing your shoulders over. It is at this stage that you can start to introduce some mobility into the stance by flexing your legs. However, do not bend your knees so far that your body drops. Having "sat down" you will find the incorrect angle of your spine misdirects the plane of the swing. The result will inevitably be a mishit shot.

While achieving the ideal stance for the shot you intend to play, you must continuously check the club so that the bottom edge of the club-head is always square to the ball and relating to the target. It is at this stage that you should take up the grip.

*Although you should always adopt a posture that is flexed and relaxed, you must never allow your body to slouch. When playing with a long iron (ABOVE RIGHT), you should have the feeling of standing tall.*

*Even though the reduced shaft of the shorter irons (RIGHT) brings you more over the top of the ball, resulting in a more rounded look to the shoulders, you should retain the feeling of keeping your head up.*

*The angle of the shoulders will vary according to the type of club being used. When playing with the driver, which has the longest shaft of all the clubs, and with the ball well forward in the stance (FAR LEFT), the shoulders must be allowed to adopt quite a marked slant to permit the head to remain central in the stance. With one of the middle irons (BELOW LEFT) the slant is still evident. But because the shaft is shorter and the ball is further back in the stance, the slant is less obvious. When playing with a short iron (LEFT), where the shaft is shorter still and the ball is positioned centrally in the stance, there is only a trace of a slant in the shoulders.*

## The grip

It is important to remember when taking up the grip on the handle of the club that there are two definite stages involved – passing the club to the left hand and then bringing across the right hand to complete the grip. The reasons for this are explained below.

Although over recent years variations in the style of the grip have been adopted, the basic elements of the modern-day grip originate from that established by Harry Vardon in the 1930s. The main alternative involves the position of the little finger of the right hand.

Whereas with the traditional Vardon grip the little finger of the right hand overlapped the forefinger of the left hand, some people now interlock the two. However, the basic principles of the Vardon grip still apply – and with them the many advantages over other unorthodox methods of holding the club-handle.

The most important aspect of the grip is that it should enable both hands to work in unison and, at the same time, allow them to perform their own specific jobs. At the risk of oversimplifying the situation, in essence the left hand should be used to provide the support and authority required to control the swing. The right hand should remain sufficiently sensitive to administer whatever finesse or, in some cases, power that is needed to create the right "touch" for the shot being played. Before discussing in detail how the ideal grip is achieved, it is worth looking more closely at the left and right hands and what they should – and should not – be doing.

As far as the left hand is concerned, it is the top part of the palm and the fingers that do the majority of the gripping. When the grip is tightened, the tension runs up the inside of the arm and it is the muscles here that actually take most of the strain when the club is being swung back, then down and into the strike. What is particularly important is that this left hand position does not restrict the wrist from cocking and uncocking freely, as it must do during the swing and when the ball is struck.

The difference between the left hand grip and that of the right is a marked and important one. In fact the grip provided by the right hand should be virtually all in the fingers – and hardly at all in the palm. Looking at it another way, you could think of the left hand as being the dull provider of authority, while the right hand introduces flair and variety.

With much of the early work, the right hand follows the demands of the left. But as the club-head nears the strike, the right hand takes on a distinctive role of its own since it is the hand that helps control the club-head into the ball.

In order to insure that you adopt your grip on the club correctly every time you play a shot, think about it as a two-stage action and go through each stage carefully.

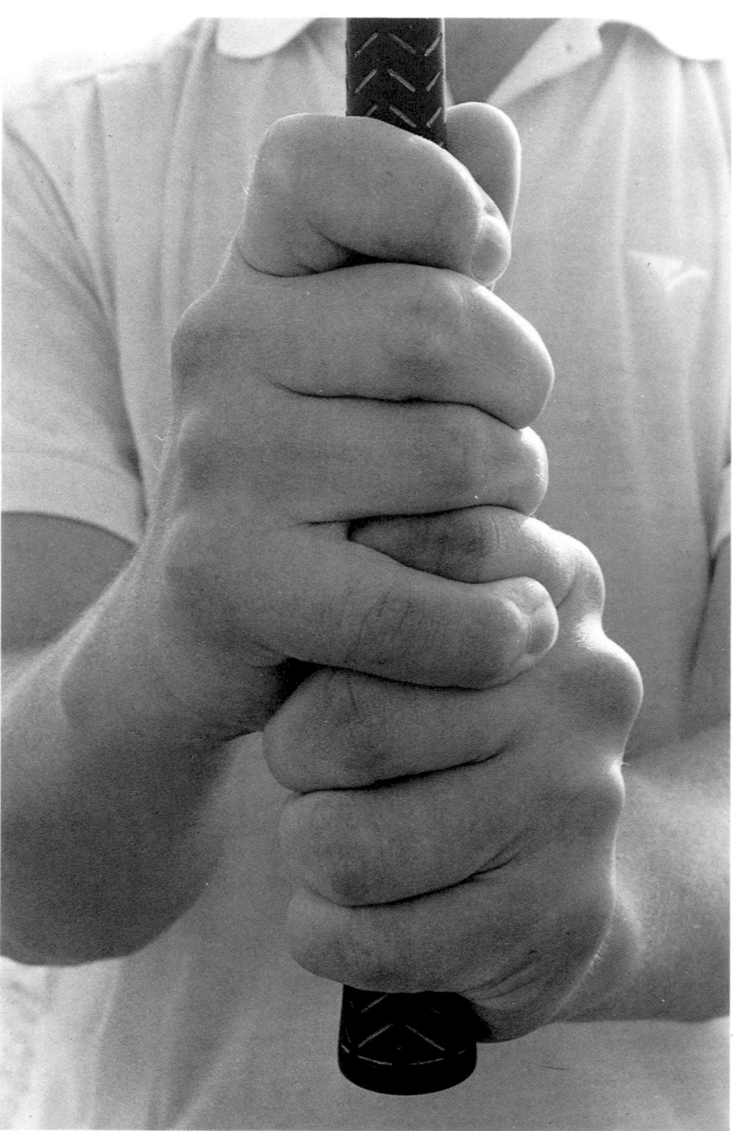

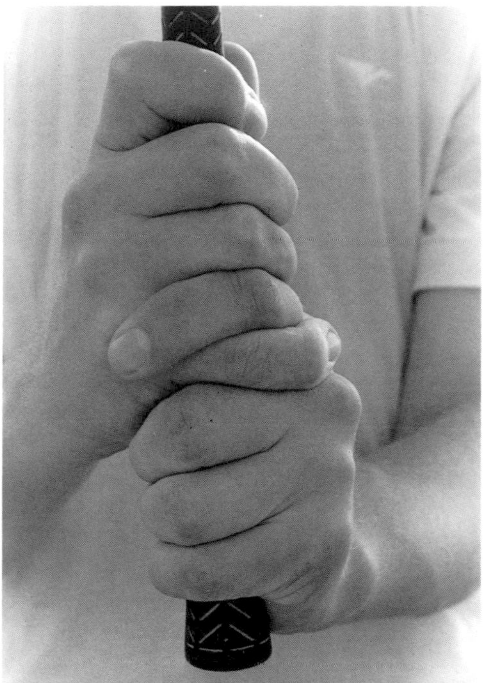

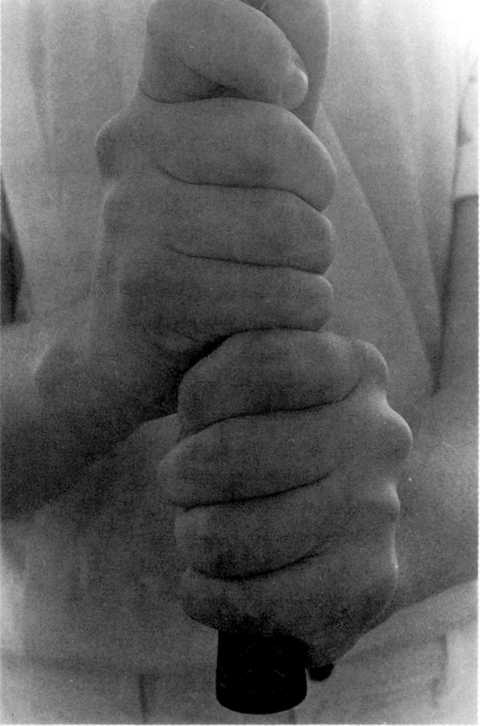

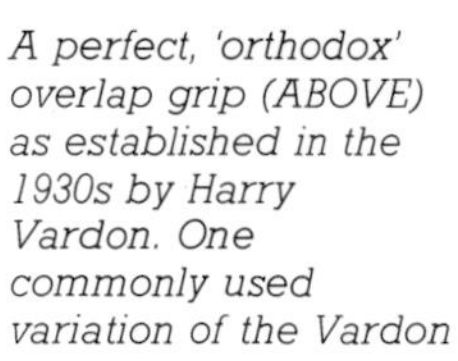

*A perfect, 'orthodox' overlap grip (ABOVE) as established in the 1930s by Harry Vardon. One commonly used variation of the Vardon grip (ABOVE RIGHT) is where the index finger of the left hand and the little finger of the right hand interlock rather than overlap. The 'baseball' grip (RIGHT), where all the fingers are on the handle of the club, is often advised for children or ladies with small hands.*

**Stage One** The first stage in taking up the correct grip is to pass the club from your right hand into your left, which should be in line with your left leg. One of the basic elements in successful swinging is to coordinate the overall movements of those parts of the body involved in the swing. This means that your body, arms, wrists and hands should all work together and not independently. By feeling the left arm and wrist forward opposite the left leg when the grip is taken up, all will then be able to move smoothly into the swing.

If you bring your left hand towards the club – that is, in a more central position in the stance – your left wrist will automatically be hinged in the opposite direction. When you start your back swing, your left hand will have to straighten out before it can follow the swing movement naturally. This will involve you in more wrist and hand movement, but less body, arm and shoulder movement. As a result, your shoulders will not turn as much as they should into the back swing. (Remember, the shoulders are crucial in effecting a successful swing.) Consequently your body – including your shoulders – will be ahead of the club in the down swing.

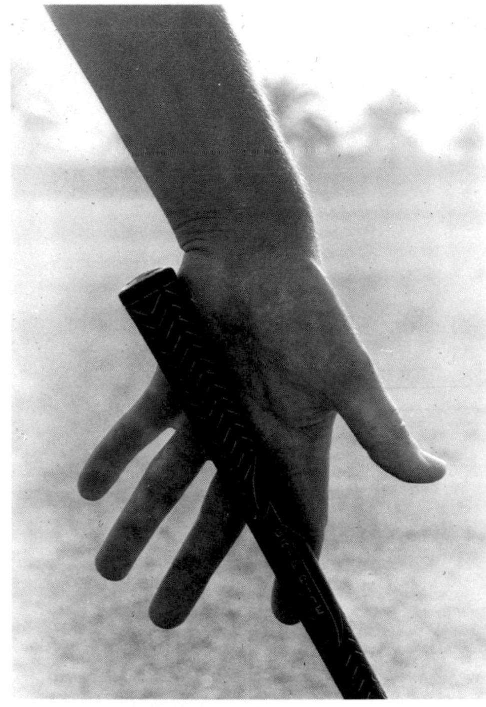

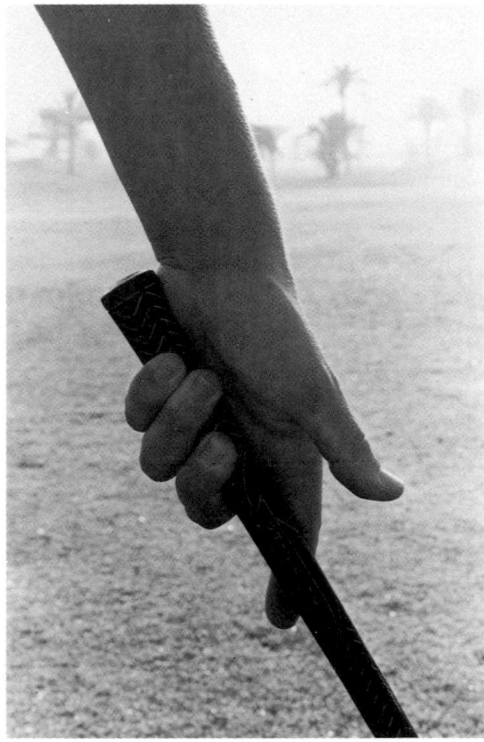

*The angle at which the shaft of the club passes down through the left hand (ABOVE RIGHT) enables the club to become an extension of the left arm. During the swing the greatest pressure on the hands affects the end fingers of the left hand. You should apply the primary pressure at this point when you first take up the grip (RIGHT).*

*The placing of the forefinger and thumb (ABOVE) onto the handle (so the thumb is only slightly to the right of center) is very important for it must allow the right hand room in which to fit over. There should be an impression of pulling the left thumb upward.*

The net result of this is normally a slice off to the right. This happens because the face of the club-head is open and trailing behind the body as it returns toward the intended point of impact.

Although this sounds rather complicated, the best way to understand it is to practice the swing from both situations. First bring your left hand back to a central position to take up the grip. Then bring the club forward with your right hand to a forward left arm and wrist position. When you attempt to swing in slow motion, using the two left hand positions in turn, you will notice the difference. This will be highlighted when you bring the club-head down and into the strike. What you need to insure is that the outside of your hand and forearm are facing square on to the target throughout the taking up of the grip.

Depending on the type of shot you are planning to play, the angle of the club-handle across the palm of your left hand will vary. The greater the angle when using longer clubs, the less your left thumb will be extended down the handle. In contrast, the shorter the club the less the angle of the handle across the palm and therefore the further your left thumb will reach down the shaft.

**Stage Two** This involves bringing the right hand over to take up its grip on the club-handle. Under normal circumstances you should never alter the position of your left hand when doing this. (There are very few exceptions to this – the most important will be discussed later, see p. 182.)

It is equally vital that you should not attempt to grip with the palm of your right hand since it is only through the use of a finger grip with your right hand that any degree of finesse can be applied to the shot. When bringing your right hand across to the club-handle, open it out and make sure it remains square to and facing the target.

Depending on the exact position of your left hand in the grip – which will be determined by the type of shot being played – the position of your right hand will also vary slightly. Use your right forefinger to hook around the club-handle, with your thumb helping to support it. This will provide the perfect conditions for fitting your left-hand thumb on top of the handle. Then the two center

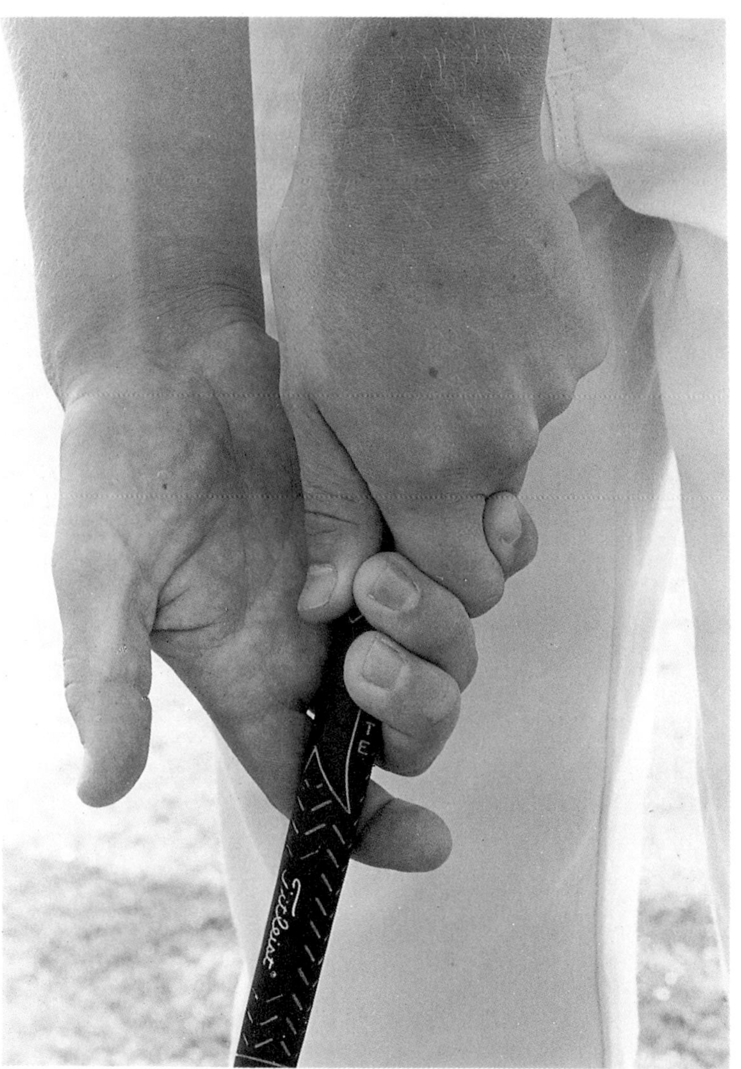

*From this angle (ABOVE) you can clearly see the benefit of placing the left hand correctly on the handle, making it easy for the right hand, which basically adopts a finger grip, to be applied. The middle two fingers, which are formed into the shape of a trough, are positioned on the handle close up against the left hand. It is at this stage that the little finger of the right hand creates its overlap with the index finger of the left hand.*

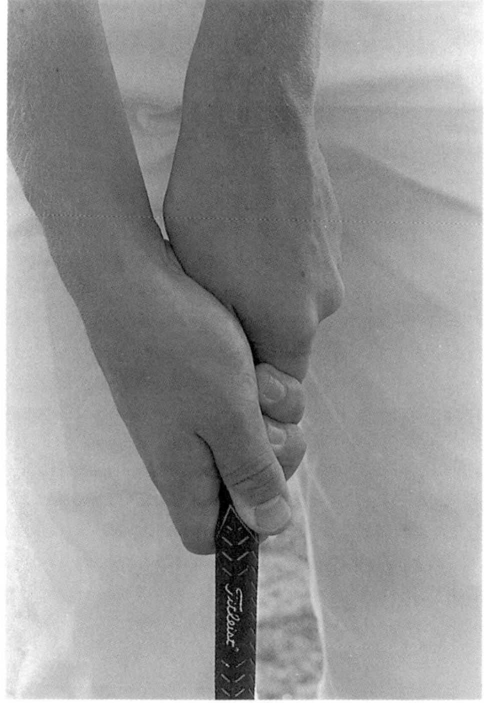

fingers together form a trough into which the handle settles. They provide the strength of the right hand.

It is worth remembering, when applying the right hand, that with most clubs your right forearm should not rise above the left. The only exceptions to this arise with the shorter clubs, particularly when you are playing a pitch shot. Here you may find that your right forearm is marginally higher than your left.

Having assumed this grip, you will discover that you have a finger left over – the little finger of the right hand. You must decide whether to overlap it with the forefinger of your left hand or interlock it. While many players with small hands claim that they prefer the interlocking method, there is no doubt that by overlapping your little finger a definite feeling of strength and support in the grip can be sensed. This is, however, a question that you will have to make up your own mind about. (It should be noted that overlapping does not damage the stability of the left hand, while interlocking can often do so.)

*When the forefinger and thumb of the right hand are placed on the handle (ABOVE LEFT) a V shape is formed that points in the direction of the right shoulder. This matches that of the left hand, insuring that the two palms are parallel, which is an essential element of correct swinging.*

*It is clear from this view of the Vardon grip (LEFT) how the benefits are derived. The left hand, with a palm and finger hold, offers stability while the right hand, with its finger grip, benefits from the sensitive feel essential for that all-important, delicate touch.*

## The swing

The greatest mistake beginners make when learning the swing is to break it down into separate actions. By practicing stage-by-stage the backward, forward and through movements, you will already have destroyed any chance of a continuous, fluent action which is vital for consistent, accurate swinging. Although the complete swing is made up of different parts of the body working in their own way, they must act in perfect harmony. While checking that each is performing as it should, you should always practice the swing in its entirety.

The whole point of the swing is to send the ball where you want it and in the way you want it. Never lose sight of this objective. To this end, it is what the club-head does that is so crucial, since its contact with the ball will determine what the ball does afterwards. You must, therefore, concentrate on what the club-head is doing throughout the swing, since if this is following the correct path at the correct angle and with the correct pace, the impression gained is that the body and arms are naturally moving in sympathy, rather than leading the club.

The accuracy and success of your swing will depend to a great extent on the overall posture you adopt. It is vital, therefore, that attention is given to getting your stance right. This includes the position of the ball, the distance away from it that you stand and the line you take with your feet.

Having taken care to get the stance right, there are several other parts of the body that you must also pay specific attention to – the hands and wrists, the shoulders and arms, and the feet and legs.

**Hands and wrists** The hands are the means through which power is passed from the forearms to the club, to enable you to swing with the right degree of

*You must never make the mistake of practicing swinging from and back to the ball. Every practice swing should be taken onto a complete follow-through position. The golden rule for all golfers is "don't swing to the ball; swing through it."*

*HANDS AND WRISTS*
*The left wrist has cocked fully and the right has hinged in agreement, enabling the shaft of the club to point toward the target while it lies virtually parallel to the ground.*

*HEAD*
*Although at this stage of the swing there is great pressure on the neck, the head has to be kept as near centrally in the stance as possible.*

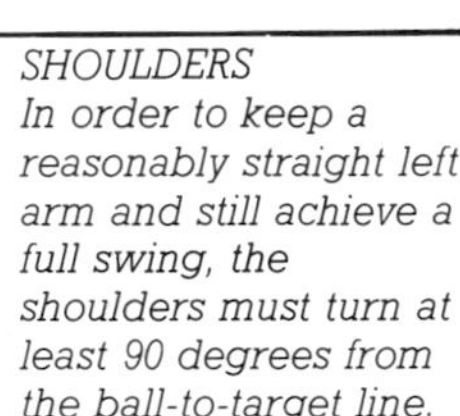

*SHOULDERS*
*In order to keep a reasonably straight left arm and still achieve a full swing, the shoulders must turn at least 90 degrees from the ball-to-target line.*

*HIPS*
*Although the hip turn is never more than half that of the shoulders, there must be free movement here as they turn into the back swing.*

*LEGS*
*It is essential that the right knee does not stiffen backward, since this will lock the swing. There should always be a feeling of flexibility in both knees.*

*FEET*
*It is advisable to allow the left heel to lift a little off the ground in the back swing. If not, it is possible to lean into the left side during the swing and this in turn will impair a good weight transfer.*

*Here the roles of the relevant parts of the body are highlighted at the top of the back swing.*

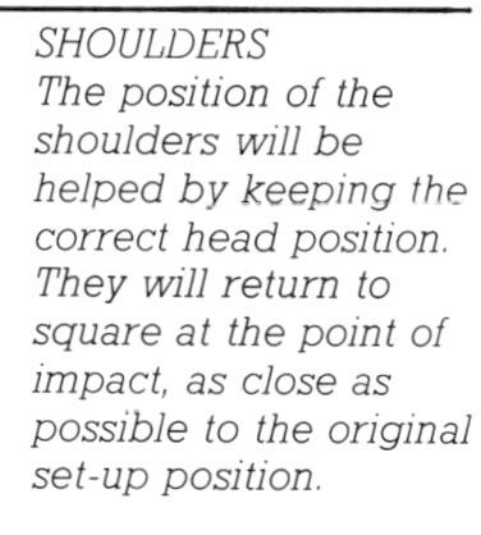

*HEAD*
*The impression you should have of remaining central in your stance while swinging can only be achieved if the head stays comparatively still above its original focus point, and is not drawn to the left with the force of aggression in the down swing.*

*ARMS*
*The right arm should always feel as though, on the down swing, it returns slightly inside the plane of the left arm.*

*HANDS*
*A good grip and correct hand preparation in the back swing will insure that you strike the ball with both hands together. There must never be a feeling that one hand is working independently of its partner.*

*SHOULDERS*
*The position of the shoulders will be helped by keeping the correct head position. They will return to square at the point of impact, as close as possible to the original set-up position.*

*HIPS*
*The left hip, which played a leading part at the start of the down swing, moves to the left and forward into the shot, at the same time preparing to clear the way for the through swing.*

*LEGS*
*The temptation to brace the left leg in the down swing should be avoided. Just as in the back swing, there should be a feeling of flexibility in the knees.*

*FEET*
*The left foot is of vital importance here, since it takes the weight of the body as it transfers to the left and establishes a degree of authority in the shot.*

*Here the roles of the relevant parts of the body are highlighted at the point of impact in the down swing.*

*HEAD*
*Although the head has been allowed to turn freely to look after the ball, it still retains the central position it adopted at the set-up.*

*ARMS*
*The complete follow-through, with the hands and arms high in the swing, should be held long into the ball's flight. Any collapse here will have a very poor long-term effect on the golf swing.*

*HIPS*
*The pelvis should now be facing directly toward the target.*

*LEGS*
*The right leg must be released freely into the follow-through to allow the body to turn after the shot has been played, and help give greater length to the flight of the ball.*

*LEFT FOOT*
*With the left foot, the entire weight of the body should be on the outside edge of the sole of the shoe. But the authority of the shot should still be there and on no account should there be any spinning of the foot.*

*RIGHT FOOT*
*With the body weight by now completely off the right side, the only contact with the ground here should be the very tip of the shoe. From behind, all the spikes in the shoe should be visible.*

*Here the roles of the relevant parts of the body are highlighted at the end of the follow-through.*

*At the top of the back swing, the left wrist must cock so that an angle of at least 90 degrees between the shaft and the forearm is formed (RIGHT). With the palms of each hand parallel, the right wrist finds it very easy to hinge backward.*

strength. However, their most important role is to control the line and angle of the swing. This is not nearly so evident or crucial when playing a full-blooded shot, since having got into the correct posture and mastered the basic swing techniques you should, with constant practice, be able to play this type of shot again and again without consciously creating too much activity in the hands and wrists.

This does not mean that they do not have a job to do. Where the work of the hands and wrists becomes more evident – and, in fact, is vital for the success of the stroke – is when you are playing the shorter, more delicate shots such as the pitch or chip.

The basic sequence through which the hands and wrists move during the swing begins with the back swing. By the time you have reached the top of the back swing your left wrist should be cocked back to create at least a right angle between the left arm and the shaft of the club. The more power you want to put into the shot, the greater the angle you will cock your wrist. While it is very important that you do cock the wrist fully, it is dangerous to overstrain this, since the wrist will then collapse. The advantage here of a finger grip on the club-handle with the right hand becomes obvious since, while the fingers are maintaining their control over the club, the hands remain flexible enough at the wrist to hinge back as required.

Having reached the correct position with your hands and wrists at the top of the back swing, the next movement requires great skill. While both your left and right wrists must straighten out during the down swing, the timing of this in relation to the striking of the ball is critical. Your hands must return to their original position in the set-up stage as the club is playing through the ball. This

*Continual practice at swinging through the base of the arc not only leads to a better sense of timing but also demonstrates the simple process of the hands, wrists and arms passing the club-head through the ball. At the stage shown here (TOP), as the forearms part-rotate toward the ball, the hands and wrists are almost completely uncocked. By the point of impact (CENTER) you can see how close the player is to his original set-up position. The forearms and hands are simply sweeping the club-head through its original swingbase, almost relying on the weight transfer to the left side to give momentum to the shot. Finally the forearms are allowed to part-rotate naturally in the opposite direction (BOTTOM) and the hands and wrists begin to fold toward the follow-through position.*

is pretty well impossible to check when you are actually hitting a shot, because of the speed at which the club is traveling into the strike. By swinging down in slow motion you will get some idea of whether your hands are reasonably in position. But the only accurate way of telling is to strike the ball and see what line it takes.

If you straighten your wrists too soon, before you reach the point of impact, the tendency will be to swing the club outside the intended line of the shot. This will result in the ball starting its journey to the left of the target. If, on the other hand, your hands have not reached their original position when you come to strike the ball, you will tend to swing the club across the line of the shot from the inside. This will result in the ball starting its journey to the right of the target.

While the exact timing of this hand and wrist movement is important to insure accurate striking of the ball – and one you should spend a lot of time perfecting – you must avoid becoming static in the hitting area. All practice swings should be continued through to a full follow-through position.

**Shoulders and arms** While these parts of the body have their own specific jobs to do during the swing – and should therefore function independently – it is absolutely essential that their individual movements are coordinated so that they produce a smooth swing. This means they should both have reached their respective positions by the time you have got to the top of your back swing. Equally, all through the down swing they must work in unison.

The effectiveness of the shoulders in the swing will depend on whether you have adopted the correct posture in the first place. This relates to your distance from the ball and how much you bend your spine forward, depending on the club being used. This, as already stated, will determine the plane of the swing.

The back swing provides the "wind up" for the eventual shot, and at its height you should find that it is the muscles down the left side of your body that are starting to pull. To achieve this, it is your left shoulder that you should turn, taking the right with it so that your shoulders are rounded.

When swinging into the point of strike, however, it is the power from the right side of your body – and, in particular, your right shoulder – that provides much of the strength for the shot.

The exact amount of work required of the arms will depend on the type of shot and therefore the type of club being used. With the shorter irons, the wrists tend to do most of the work, whereas the arms really come into their own for full-blooded shots with the longer irons and, in particular, the woods. As the arc of the swing increases, added demands are placed on the arms to provide extra power and fullness of arc in the shot.

One aspect of the movement of the arms has simplified that all-important part of the swing – hitting the ball cleanly and squarely with the face of the club-head. It is simpler because it is a natural movement. Traditionally on the down swing a good deal of conscious wrist work was used to turn the club-face, in order that it could meet the ball square on. With the swing techniques now adopted, where the left wrist is cocked true to the swing of the left arm, and not outward from that direction, this is no longer necessary.

What in effect happens is that the forearms rotate partially in a clockwise direction as the club is brought up in the back swing. This rotation is then reversed as the club is swung down and into the strike, so that at the point of impact the forearms have returned to their original position.

The easiest way to demonstrate this point is to hold out your hands, with the palms facing each other. Then turn your forearms clockwise through 90 degrees.

*As you reach the top of the back swing, your left shoulder is pulled completely around to the front so that it lies between your chin and the ball (LEFT). Although the hips should move freely, they must never turn more than half the turn of the shoulders. If they do, you will lose that feeling of "winding up" and find that you are spinning rather than turning into the swing.*

At this stage your left palm will be facing down and your right palm facing up. This is what happens in the back swing, before the rotation is reversed during the down swing and they return to their original position at the point of impact.

**Feet and legs** Despite the fact that the basic control of the club – and therefore the ball – comes through the top half of the body, it is the bottom half of the body that looks after the important transfer of weight and overall balance. Without these, all the good work put into the swing would be wasted.

While your body weight is transferred toward the right side during the back swing, it should be thought of as swing pressure rather than weight. You turn as the weight is transferring. If, therefore, you move your weight over to the right side laterally, you create a severe sway to the right. Swaying for weight transfer will drain the left side of the body of its authority and you will find yourself stuck back on your right foot for the down swing.

The weight of the body during the back swing turns to the right side. This is then transferred back to the left side during the down swing and through the strike. The secret is to try to keep the body as level as possible through the back swing and into the down swing and avoid all feeling of dipping. There are two basic ways in which this can be achieved. The first and simplest is to lift the heel of the left foot off the ground during the back swing. The second and harder method is to maintain the bend of the right knee, which was part of the setting up. This will prove more difficult because it is this leg that takes most of the weight of your body at this stage in the swing.

One of the key ingredients of a correct swing is keeping all the various movements as fluid as possible, despite the fact that at the top of the back swing you are required to change direction. In this respect the legs are no different to the other moving parts of the body. The greatest danger when reaching the top of the back swing is to lock the right leg, which will in effect destroy the smooth flow of the movements in the preparation and execution of the swing.

*There are some extremely supple golfers who may find it possible to complete the back swing movement without lifting their left heel off the ground. For others, it is in fact of benefit to do so (INSET). If the left leg bends more than the right, which it does, but the heel does not lift then inevitably the weight will lean heavily onto the left side during the back swing, thus making it virtually impossible to complete.*

By keeping the right knee flexed during the back swing you can, on the down swing, make sure that you bring it in to provide maximum power in the strike. By doing this you will insure that the hips continue their movement back to their original position at the strike, and continue their full turn through to completion.

One interesting point to note here is the effect the position of the right side of your body – and, in particular, the right knee – has on the type of shot finally played. The earlier and further forward you bring your right knee in with the strike, the higher the ball will fly. Equally, by holding it back, the ball will travel on a lower trajectory.

*Here you can see clearly the ideal leg and foot action during the complete swing sequence (RIGHT), with the build-up of power under control toward the top of the back swing, and then the balanced journey of the club down into and through the point of impact, and finally the complete, free release of the swing to the finish of the follow-through.*

## Swing plane

This is the angle at which the club is swung back and then down through the strike. It is determined by several factors – the player's build, the type of club and the slope of the ground, if any. As a general rule, with standard length clubs, the longer the club the flatter the angle of the swing; while the shorter the club the steeper the angle.

This does not mean, however, that every golfer has to learn a different angle for each of the clubs in the set. Provided that the correct set-up has been achieved, the length of the club will determine the swing plane by bringing the spine further forward or keeping it more upright, whatever the case may be. This is why the posture is such an important aspect of successful golf.

You must always bear in mind that the perfect swing should appear to be in a straight line, looking from the side of the player – that is, from behind the line of the shot. This means that when you draw the club back to the top of the back swing and then bring it down to the strike and on into the through swing, you must maintain as near as possible the same swing plane.

This is in complete contrast to the original concept of the swing, whereby the club was first brought inwards on the back swing and then raised up above the shoulders. The secret of successful swinging is to bring the club up behind you in the back swing and then down into the through swing with an awareness of one direct swing plane. There should be no looping.

*It is absolutely vital that you do not try to argue with the swing plane. When you are using the long-shafted wooden clubs (ABOVE RIGHT) the angle of attack on the ball must come more from around the body. The wood will therefore have the shallowest of swing planes. With a long iron (RIGHT) the swing plane is still fairly shallow, although a touch more upright than for the wood.*

*With a wedge, it is easy to see how the swing plane is forced sharply upright (ABOVE). It is worth comparing this swing with that for the wooden club to note the two extremes.*

In order to achieve this direct simplicity in the swing, you must maintain the angle of your spine throughout the movement of the club. Once you have established this in the set-up when you adopt your posture, you should hold it in the back swing and on into the down swing – and even into the follow-through.

To demonstrate exactly how the swing plane works, the following exercise – which does not involve the use of a club – should be practiced. Stand opposite a ball as if you were about to play with a middle iron. Stretch out both arms with the forefinger of each hand pointing at the ball. Now swing your right arm up and back until it is approximately opposite your left arm. (Make sure that you do not bend it.) From this position the angle of the swing plane required to play that particular shot can be readily seen.

To complete the exercise, bring your right arm back into its original position while at the same time pivoting your left arm forward. This movement will indicate the angle of the through swing and follow-through. By moving your arms backward and forward as described, you will get a very clear idea of the swing plane.

By moving further away from the ball and repeating this exercise, you will see how the swing plane flattens out when you use the longer clubs. Equally, by moving in a little you will see how it gets steeper with the shorter irons. Remember to keep your arms outstretched, with both forefingers initially pointing at the ball.

## Swing path

The swing path is the direction the club takes as it passes through the low point of the swing, the strike area, and on toward the follow-through. Provided that you swing the club in the same plane throughout, this path will be assisted by the line of your shoulders when you set up for the shot and by the smooth movement of your arms.

So how does this work in practice? Normally you will be aiming to strike the ball squarely with the club-face and therefore the stance you adopt should be square to the line of the shot – as will be the aim of your shoulders. This means that, if you maintain a swing path back and then down into the strike that is traveling toward the target, then you will achieve what is known as a *direct swing path.* There are times, however, when more experienced players will want to vary the line of their swing path. This happens when for one reason or another they want to curve the shot – either to the left or to the right. In either case, they will then need to bring the club-head through to the strike from one side of the target line and carry on through to the other side of this line. To do this, a slightly different set-up position is needed for the shot.

Let us first consider the example of

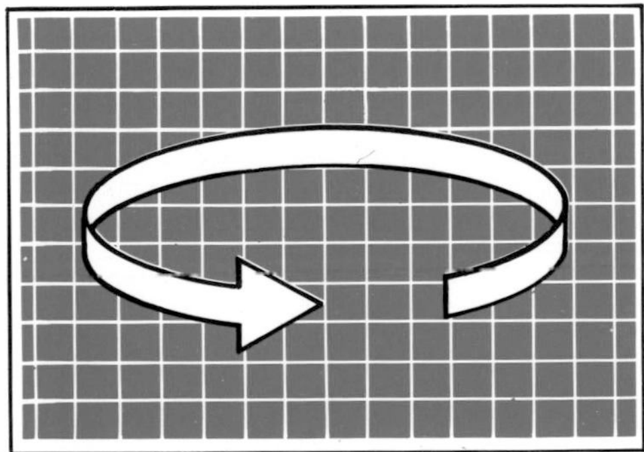

*This sequence shows the direct swing path. The aerial view (LEFT) shows that the club does actually travel inward from the ball-to-target line, both in the back and through swing. Nevertheless, at the top of the back swing the shaft lies true to the target, just as it does at that point of the swing before the wrists finally buckle into the follow-through position. When playing a direct shot toward the target, you should feel that the club is working on a straight line through the area of impact (BELOW). This impression is gained because everything in the set-up was parallel to the ball-to-target line and consequently the swing was directed to the target.*

someone wanting to send the ball off to the right and then curve it back into the left. In this case the club needs to follow what is described as an *in-to-out* swing path. This means that on the down swing the club will be traveling from somewhere between the body and the line of the shot – that is, inside the target line – and will continue on across that line to the outside, hence the expression in-to-out.

This technique is achieved by bringing your left shoulder further across in front of you and nearer to the line of the shot, and involves positioning the ball further back in the stance. In this situation, you would be described as having

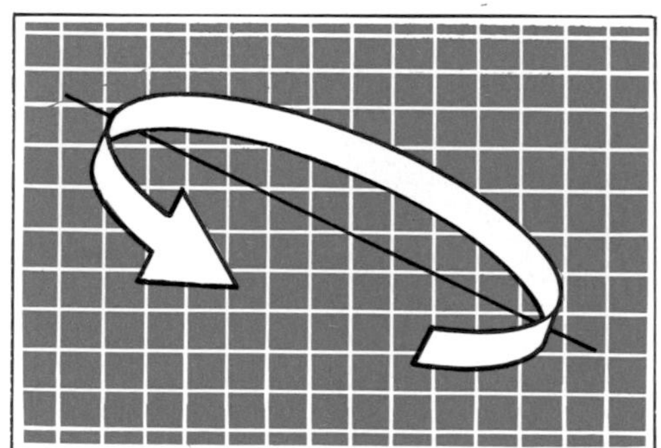

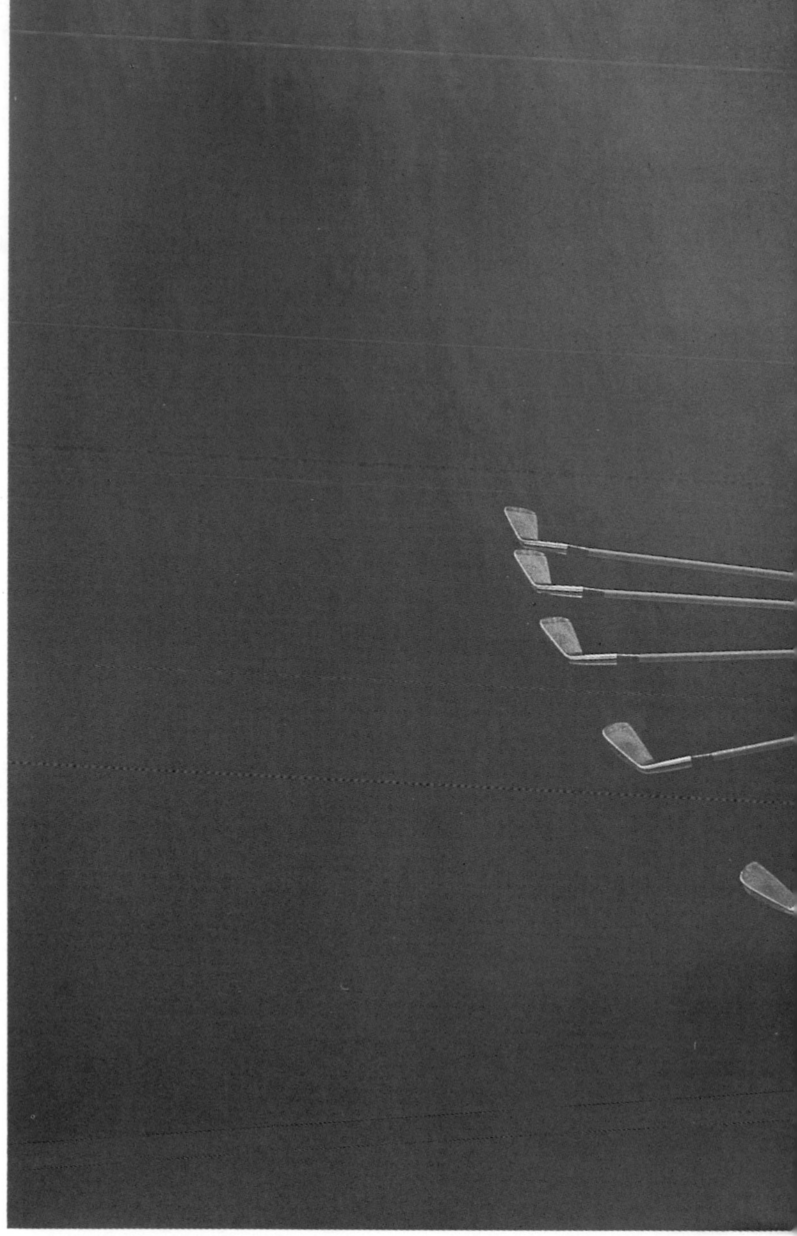

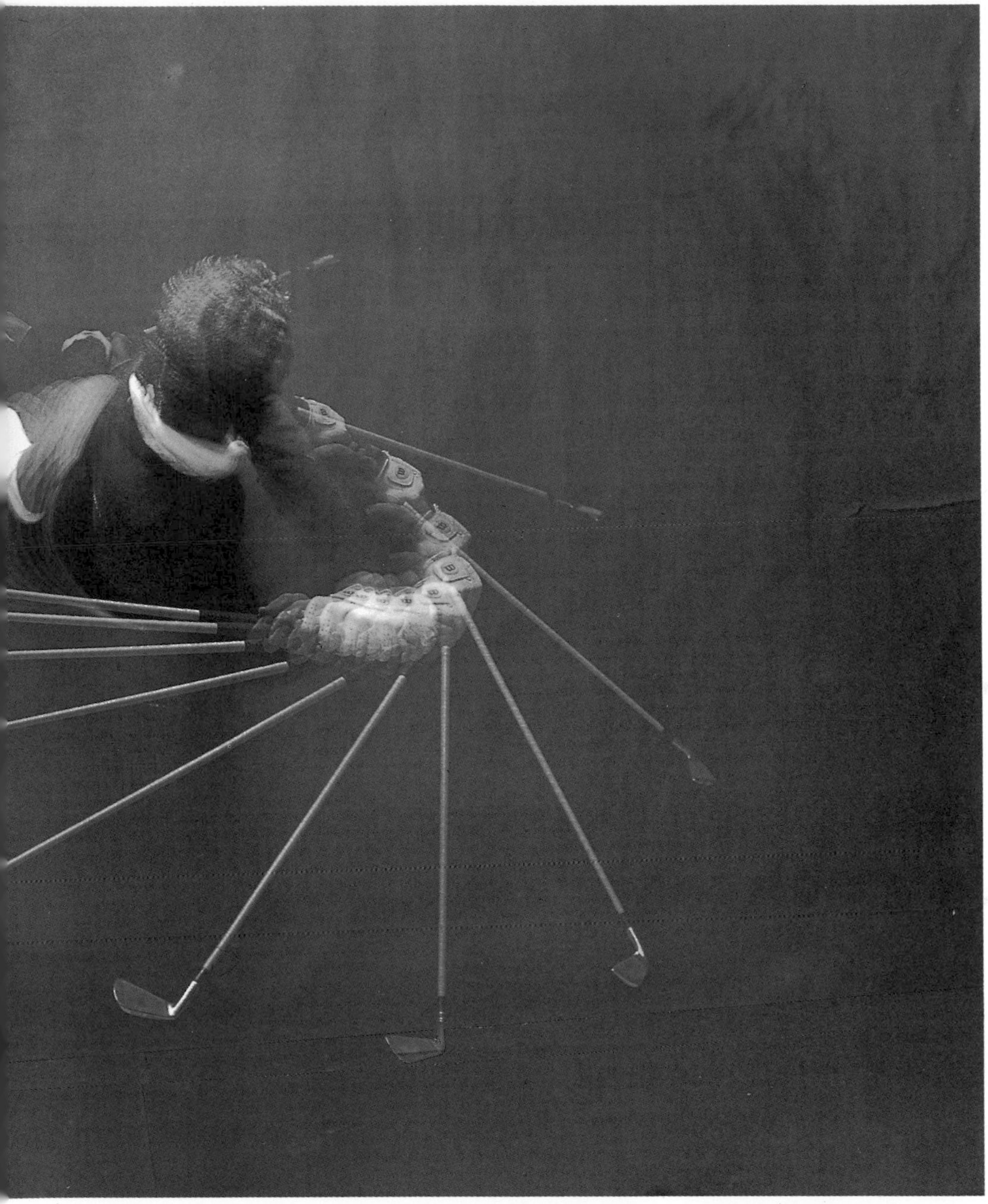

*This sequence shows the in-to-out swing path. On those occasions when you want to spin the ball in the air from right to left—i.e. a draw or hook spin shot—it is essential to alter the swing path of the club from the target line. By adjusting the set-up position, it is a simple matter to change the swing path of the club so that it travels more sharply inward from the ball-to-target line during the back swing. This in turn makes it possible for you to swing the club down and out across that ball-to-target line in the through swing.*

*This sequence shows the out-to-in swing path. When you want to hit a shot that spins from left to right—as in the case of a fade or slice—the alteration to the set-up is made so that the left side of the body opens away from the ball-to-target line.*

*The restricted movement of the back swing causes the club to come back outside the ball-to-target line. This then leaves it a downward journey across this imaginary target line from outside to in.*

closed your shoulders for the shot.

Now consider the reverse situation, where the player wants to send the ball off to the left and then curve it back into the right. The route the club must take would in this case be described as an *out-to-in* swing path, where the club on the down swing starts on the far side of the target line and is brought across it and inside on the follow-through.

To achieve this, your right shoulder must be nearer to the line of the shot than your left shoulder, and the ball must be positioned further forward in the stance. This is known as having opened your shoulders for the shot.

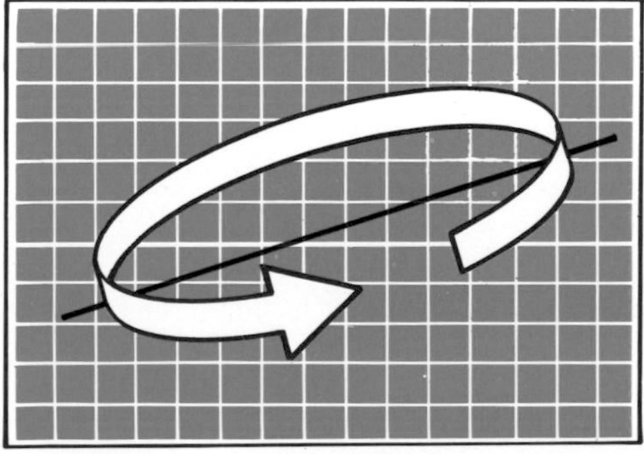

*There can be no questioning the fact that the swing path of the club is dictated by the shoulder line, whether this is done intentionally or by accident. Here you can see how the shoulder line varies according to the selected swing path as the club is moved from the ball to the top of the back swing, proving how essential it is to develop a good swing around the correct posture and set-up position.*

*The benefits of a square stance and good shoulder position (ABOVE) are clear, showing how the swing can work to the top with the club on a line parallel to the ball-to-target line.*

*With the stance closed (ABOVE RIGHT), the shoulder line at the set-up was obviously turned from the target and the club therefore crosses the line at the top of the swing.*

*Where the stance and shoulder line are open from the target (RIGHT), the sharpness of the upswing, combined with the limited amount of turn available in the shoulders, means the shaft of the club is unable to come to a position parallel with the ball-to-target line.*

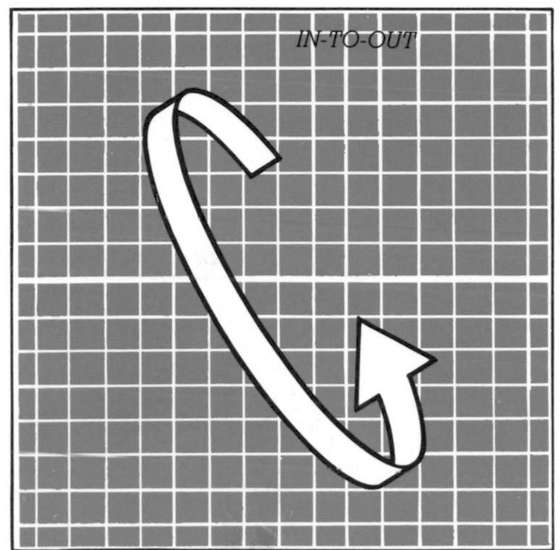
IN-TO-OUT

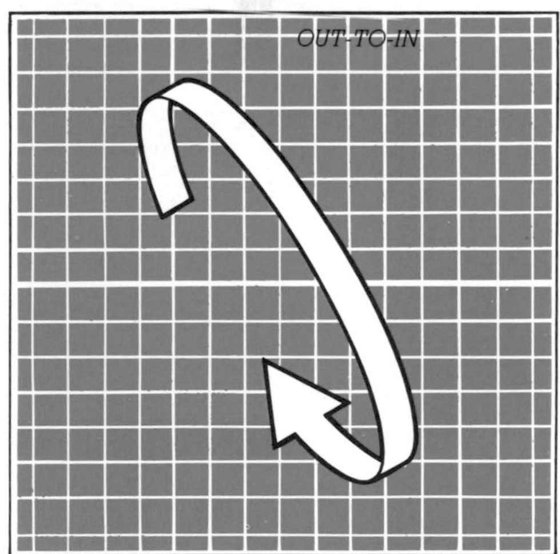
OUT-TO-IN

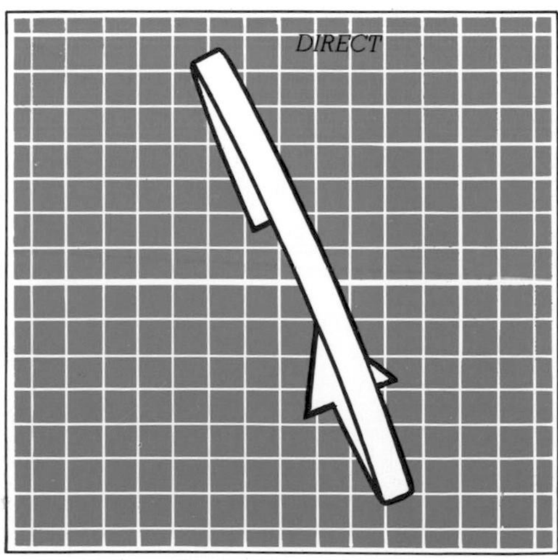
DIRECT

*Seen from behind, the effect of the body line on the swing path can be carefully studied. Having set up for the shot with the shoulder line closed (FAR LEFT), the path of the back swing is immediately committed to the inside and therefore the downward through swing is forced to cross the ball-to-target line from in to out.*

*With a set-up position where the shoulder line is aimed to the left (BOTTOM LEFT), the shaft of the club moves up on the outside, causing a very sharp upward angle of swing. The club never gets behind the body and the angle of attack on the ball is therefore a steep one, traveling across the ball-to-target line from out to in.*

*With a correct set-up (LEFT), the club can attack by traveling on the ball-to-target line through the crucial area at the base of the swing where it makes contact with the ball.*

## Practicing the swing

So far you have been shown the principles of setting up for the shot and how the various parts of the body are involved in the swing itself. You should be aware of the elements needed to perform the basic swing, when playing a ball squarely along the line of the shot with a direct swing path. Variations on this standard action will be explained later, but it is most important that you understand and master this initial golfing movement.

Now is the time to settle down and practice these elementary principles, since if you are unable to master them then any attempt to move on to the more complicated types of shot will be a complete waste of time. While you may occasionally fluke a difficult shot, you will never be in a position to guarantee its success.

There are basically five techniques that you need to rehearse and, hopefully, perfect: positioning the ball correctly, taking up the right stance, gripping the club, executing the back swing and , finally, swinging down and through the strike. Unfortunately none of these can be taken in isolation, since the success of each is dependent on getting the previous stage right. But you must, in practicing the total routine, pay attention to how you formulate each stage. This will enable you to go back afterward and recognize what you did right or wrong and, where necessary, correct your mistake.

On the basis that you will be practicing to strike the ball cleanly and squarely down the target line, with the club swinging in a direct path, choose a suitable target some distance away. This should not at this stage be within reach, since you should be solely concerned with direction and not with length. Having established a reasonable degree of consistency with the direction of your shots, you can then start to develop more power and therefore greater length in your striking.

The ideal club to practice with is one of the middle irons – a No. 5 or 6 – since these have an average degree of loft. If you choose a shorter club with more loft, you will soon develop a chopping action as your body is pulled more over the club and you will be unable to cultivate a really fluid swinging action.

**Ball position** To begin with, always take up your stance with the ball just forward of center. You can practice with the ball further forward later on. Choose a reasonable piece of ground which will give you a decent lie. If necessary, you can always set the ball up on a short tee peg.

**Stance** Establish clearly in your mind the line of the shot. If you have difficulty doing this, you can always use a visual aid such as a club or a length of tape laid parallel to your intended target. This is important, because when you adopt your stance you must insure that your whole body is facing this target line square on

One excellent discipline is to spend some time looking along the line of the shot to the target. For this you should only turn your head and *never* twist your body. Having set up your stance square to the line of the shot, if you do then turn your body at all it is likely that you will not return to exactly the same position. The more you turn to check on the target, the more you will move your stance out of its square on position.

When you take up your stance, remembering to place the right foot first, make sure that you lean over slightly toward the ball. You are bound to make mistakes to begin with when judging the distance between yourself and the ball, but with practice your judgment will become more accurate. It is far better to learn the correct posture – even at the wrong distance – than to start playing all your shots from an upright position or leaning back slightly.

*While laying a club on the ground parallel to the ball-to-target line (ABOVE) is not allowed during actual play on the course, it does provide a very good practice method when setting up for the shot.*

*Learning to line up the blade of the club simultaneously with the right foot being correctly placed (TOP RIGHT) is one of the greatest aids to accurate aiming. Checking this aim should be done by turning the head and not by twisting the body.*

*Initial efforts to line up the right foot and the club together often cause you to stand too close to the ball when the left foot is brought forward (RIGHT). Only through continual practice can the distance be judged correctly.*

*Placing the handle of the club against the left hand by holding it with the forefinger and thumb of the right hand (RIGHT) makes you aware that the back of the left hand and forearm are directly facing the target. Then, when the left hand completes its grip (FAR RIGHT), there is a strong relationship between the face of the club and the back of the left hand.*

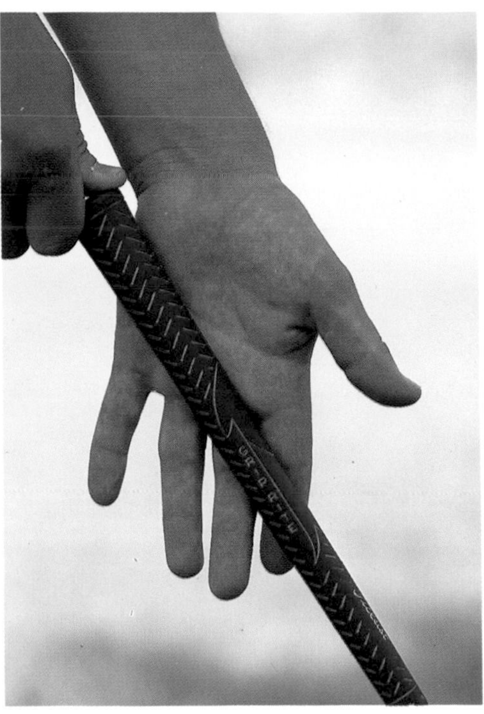

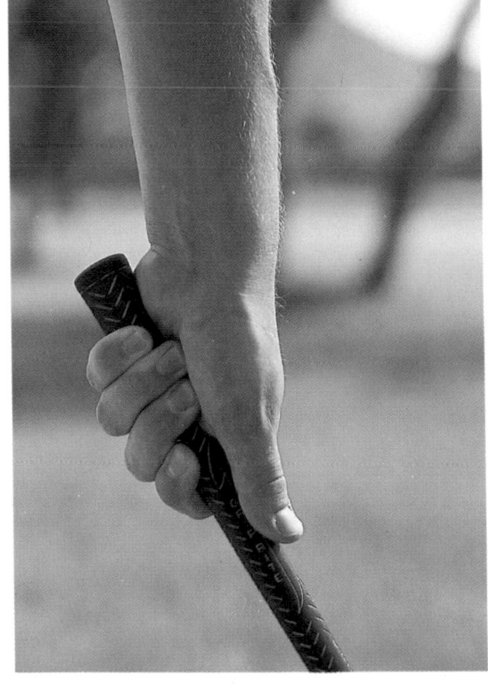

**Grip** Taking up the correct grip will never be easy for the beginner, since it is bound initially to feel very awkward. However, you must persevere with it, remembering to introduce the club to your left hand, which should be held just in front of the ball, and then adding your right.

A good way of checking that your hands are in the right position for the grip is to look down the shaft of the club. Provided that you have adopted the correct shoulder position, with your left shoulder slightly higher than the right and your right forearm just lower than the left, you should be able to see two and possibly three of the knuckle joints on your left hand. However, you must also check that the club-head is square to the ball and to the line of the shot.

The handle of the club should be resting comfortably in the palm of your left hand, with the right hand gripping mainly with the fingers. The position of the little finger of the right hand will depend, as already discussed, on whether you choose to overlap or interlock it.

**Back swing** The best way to perfect your back swing is to practice it in stages. Initially it is more important to pay attention to the way the club moves back and forth at the base of the swing arc, around the point of impact. The essence of accurate swinging is, after all, to hit the ball sweetly and squarely with the club-face. Even on part swings, being aware of your back swing traveling on a direct swing plane will avoid it

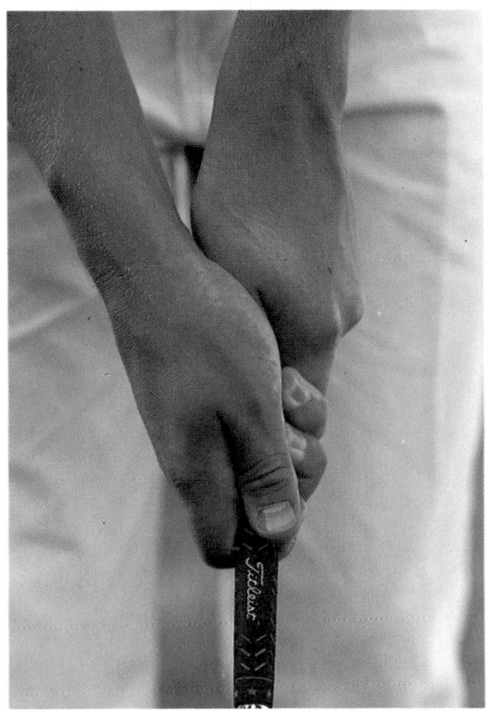

*Looking toward the hands from the target (LEFT), it should be very difficult to view the right forearm above the left. This situation is achieved by bringing the right hand up toward the left hand rather than down onto the handle of the club (FAR LEFT).*

being either lifted too sharply or swept off too wide – causing a lateral sway. This will help to insure that it does not travel back too much outside or inside the desired line. Even on smaller early shots, this allows you sufficient feel and helps develop accuracy, even if it does not send the ball any great distance.

Having mastered this movement – and that of the shoulders – as well as a very mild part-rotation of the forearms, you will find you can easily increase the extent of the back swing up to its maximum. This will also help you develop your wrist action, until you can confidently accomplish a full-strength swing into the shot.

**Through swing** The secret of successful swinging is to play through the ball and not attempt to check the forward movement after impact. The through swing is tied up with the overall body movement and transfer of weight. If this is performed correctly, the shift of weight from the right-hand side to the left-hand side of the body should naturally carry you through the shot.

As with the back swing, do not attempt to follow through too far at first and thus send yourself off balance. Build it up as the swing develops until it reaches its full extent – and remember to hold it there for a while, preferably until the ball has landed. Attempts to finish the swing with your spine still bent slightly forward will help build good golfing habits – and you may still allow your eyes to follow and enjoy the results of your shots.

*One of the best ways of establishing how far you should stand from the ball is to position the club-head behind the ball and tilt the club back so that the handle rests at the bottom of your left thigh (RIGHT).*

## Practising through the clubs

Having spent some time concentrating on all the aspects so far discussed in the development of a basic swing, the next stage is to go through the same procedure while working your way through all the clubs in the set. There are three particular points which should be noted here. The first is the varying position of the ball in relation to your stance. The second is the width of your stance (the distance apart your feet should be) and the third is the distance you should stand away from the ball.

As already mentioned, the position of the ball in relation to the stance varies from being central for the short irons to roughly opposite the left heel for the fairway woods and the driver. Likewise, for these long clubs you will need the widest stance, which should be about the same as the length of your normal walking stride. This should shorten through the clubs to just over half for the shortest iron.

When judging the distance to stand from the ball, the best guide is to place the club against the ball and then tip the shaft back until the top of the handle reaches the bottom of your left thigh. The exact distance is a matter for the individual, but this will give you a rough idea until you are in a position to judge for yourself.

## Building on the swing

You should by now have given yourself plenty of practice swinging through the range of clubs with varying lofts and watching the effects. As your confidence grows, so automatically will the length of your swing. But do not forget, as you lengthen your swing and put more power into the strike, that the same principles you have already learned still apply. You must maintain the swing path and swing plane throughout, and you must make sure that your hand and wrist

action works with the downward movement of the swing so that you strike the ball smoothly and cleanly. This can only happen if your hands and wrists straighten out into their original position at exactly the right moment – just on impact.

By extending the back swing, you will find that you are also developing the through swing to the point where the follow-through becomes automatic and the body moves fully into the final phase of the swing. Eventually, with a maximum back swing and full strength in the shot, your right foot will lift until only the toe touches the ground and your body will end up facing the target. Remember to hold that position, at least until the ball has landed.

One very important word of warning concerns the position of the head. Although, with the increased power in the swing, the shift of weight and balance will tend to force your head forward and upward into the follow-through, you should resist this until well after the ball has been struck. If not, you will find that you tend to start lifting your head earlier and earlier until eventually you take your eye off the ball and lift your head *before* completing the strike – this will almost invariably result in a badly mishit shot. Take note of how long most of the top players manage to keep their head position when playing a shot. It is a habit that is easier to develop than the other is to break.

Do not be afraid to practice with the longer clubs – in fact you should make a point of doing so. Although you are bound to mishit the shot to start with, if you keep playing safe with the shorter clubs you will never get used to coping with the longer ones. It is quite possible to be deceived by the shorter shafted, more lofted irons into believing that success is coming easily. These clubs have a degree of tolerance that longer shafted, straighter faced clubs do not possess.

*At the moment of strike (ABOVE LEFT) you can see how the left forearm and hand are well forward into the shot and there is no sign whatever of collapse. Only at a very late stage in the swing (ABOVE) should you feel that the left wrist ever gives way to the right hand.*

## Checking faults

Learning the correct techniques as already described is one thing. Knowing when and where you have gone wrong and taking the necessary steps to rectify the faults is quite another. However hard you try, in the early stages particularly – and even later on when you may think you have mastered the game – errors are bound to exist or creep into your play. The longer they go unnoticed and uncorrected, the more they will upset your play and eventually the harder they will be to put right.

In the early stages, you should be constantly aware of the possible dangers and problems and make sure you get someone who understands about golf, preferably a qualified professional coach, to have a look at your technique at regular intervals.

## Faults in the set-up

The following are the major areas in the set-up from which many golfers' problems stem.

**Aim** The most likely problems here arise from the order of doing things. You must always line up the shot and check your aim *before* you settle into your stance. The reason for this is quite simple. If you organize your set-up position *first* and then have a look to see where you are going to play the shot, you will almost certainly select the wrong position for your stance. But, even worse, you will then shuffle about in a vain attempt to correct it.

The golden rule is to establish your aim and the line of the shot first – and then take up the stance placing your right foot into position first. Leading the process by the left foot makes it difficult to achieve a good visual reference to the target, as well as having bad effects on the swing itself. By all means check your aim continually once you are over the ball by moving your head up and down along the target line, but make sure you do not move any other part of your body – from the shoulders down. If you are not happy with your aim, straighten up and start the set-up routine again from scratch.

**Ball position** Getting the ball in the correct position in relation to your stance is very important. Should you take up your stance with the ball positioned too far back you will create, depending on the

*Check the routine for the set-up carefully, since this initial preparation is vital for the success of the shot. First, simultaneously introduce the club-head to the ball and the right foot to its position (INSET). Then, when the aim is fixed, bring the left side up into position in readiness to swing the club (ABOVE).*

*The perfect ball position for an iron shot (ABOVE), where there should be no other influence on the set-up of the body other than to insure that it is square on to the ball-to-target line.*

*The effect of having the ball positioned too far back in the stance can clearly be seen (ABOVE RIGHT) as the shoulders are turned off line, definitely causing an in-to-out swing path for the club.*

*The danger of an inexperienced player using an iron with the ball too far forward in the stance (RIGHT) is that the body weight leans too much on the left leg, which will probably result in the shoulder line turning open from the target.*

*For those players who have difficulty in judging the correct position of the ball in the stance, the following set-up procedure should prove invaluable. First, line up the shot with the feet together, checking your aim by moving the head only (BELOW). Then concentrate on the ball, checking that the club-head is correctly positioned (RIGHT).*

length of swing, one of two problem situations.

If your swing is on the short side, then the club-head will be traveling across the line of the shot when it makes contact with the ball. Since the line of your shoulders will be in a more closed position, with the left shoulder pointing in toward the target line, you are bound to send the ball off to the right. With a longer swing, you could easily change the direction of the strike by means of a loop in the swing. This can have serious

repercussions in the future. In the meantime, you are very likely to bring the club-head down too steeply onto the ball.

Conversely, if you have the ball too far forward in the stance the effect is reversed. With the line of the shoulders more open, as the left shoulder is directed away from the target line, your swing will be too upright. Consequently on the down swing you will tend to hit across the target line – from outside to inside – and send the ball off to the left.

Ball position is something you will need to practice and establish for each club – the only practical method is, unfortunately, trial and error.

**Stance** Here you are likely to experience similar problems to those faced if the ball is in the wrong position. Depending on how far off line your stance is, the situation will naturally be exaggerated. As has already been stressed, you should aim to have all the relevant parts of your body in line and

*Having lined up square on to the ball-to-target line, move your left foot a little way toward the target (ABOVE LEFT) and then the right foot the same distance in the opposite direction (ABOVE). This way you will insure you achieve a central ball position.*

parallel to the target line. If your left foot and shoulder are pointing away from this line, so that you have adopted an open stance, unless you alter the position of the club-head before hitting the ball you will send it off to the left. If your left foot and shoulder are pointing inward toward the target line, your stance will be closed. Again, unless any adjustment is made to the club-head, you will strike the ball off to the right.

The important point to remember is that when you take up your stance, you must make sure that you keep those relevant parts of your body parallel to that of the target line you have *already* established.

**Distance from the ball** The distance you stand from the ball is dictated by the type of club you are using. The basic faults are caused by standing either too close or too far away from the ball. Care should be taken to cultivate a good athletic posture. You should feel balanced

*Here an evaluation can be made between the three basic set-up positions, each of which has an immediate effect on the swing path of the club. With the square stance (ABOVE RIGHT), the shoulders, forearms, hips, legs and feet are lined up parallel to the imaginary ball-to-target line.*

*With the closed stance (RIGHT), the right side of the body has been drawn back, taking the shoulders, forearms, hips, legs and feet out of line to the right.*

*When the stance is open (FAR RIGHT), the body line including the shoulders, forearms, hips, legs and feet are way off line to the left of the target.*

and just leaning slightly forward onto the balls of your feet without in any way stretching. This routine will help to insure that you stand the correct distance from the ball.

If you stand too close to the ball, you will be forced to adopt an upright stance and, in order to gain sufficient room to swing the club, you will drop back on your heels.

By standing too far from the ball, you will end up leaning so far forward that the correct balance will prove difficult to achieve and maintain. Equally your legs will not be able to play their part in producing a full, effective swing and you will have to rely almost entirely on your hands and arms. An additional problem is that you will find it virtually impossible to achieve the correct plane for the swing.

**Grip** All the control you have over the club is effected through the grip, and it is absolutely crucial if any real progress

*As well as achieving a good aim, adopting the correct posture (ABOVE LEFT) is an essential part of swinging the club accurately. The posture can easily be damaged when you are not sure how far from the ball you should stand for the shot. When standing too far away (FAR LEFT), you will bring your shoulders well forward over your feet and will thus lose the ability to turn your body in the back swing. Should you stand too close (LEFT), your body weight will sit back behind your heels and you will be committed to playing with a very flat swing.*

is to be made that you get it right. Grip problems usually stem from the position your hands take upon the club-handle, where one or other hand is too weak or too strong.

Let us look first at the problems caused by too weak a grip. With a weak left hand – where it grips too far around to the left of the handle so that hardly any knuckles are visible – you will find your left arm too weak to support the back swing. To cure this, the tendency is to move the left arm over which, if care is not taken, turns the club-face open and therefore out of line. A similar effect is caused when the right hand grip is also "weak," where it also grips too far around to the left of the handle.

With a stronger grip, the situation is in effect reversed. If your left hand is too far around to the right of the handle so that several knuckles are visible, the club-face is then in danger of being turned into a closed position. When you strike the ball it will tend to shoot off to

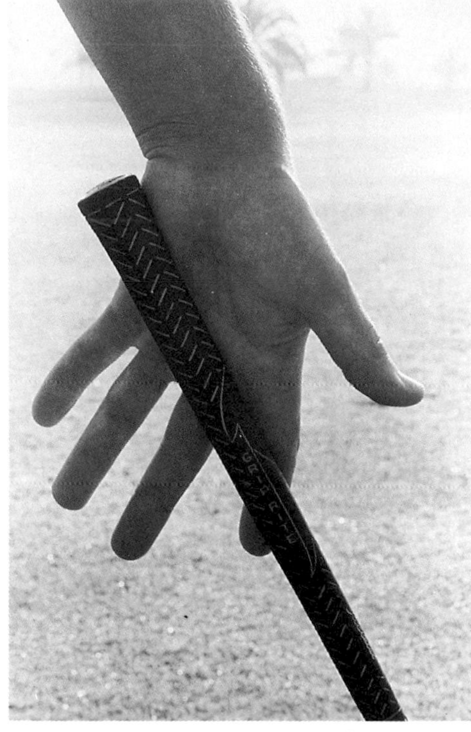

*The position of the handle in the left hand (LEFT) will dictate whether the player adopts a weak, strong or correct grip.*

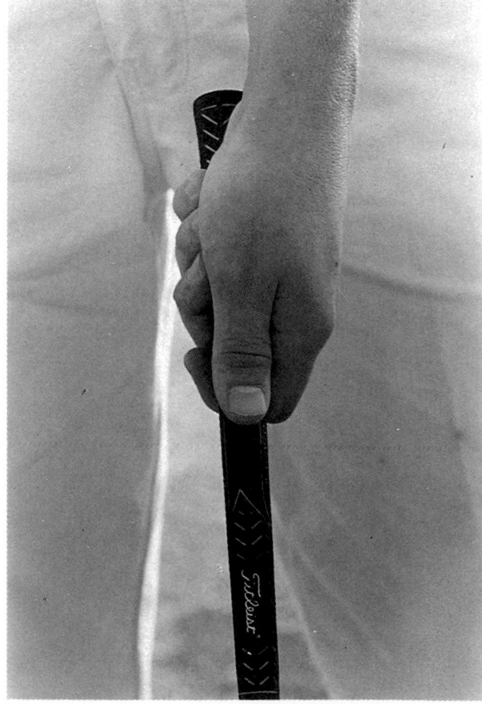

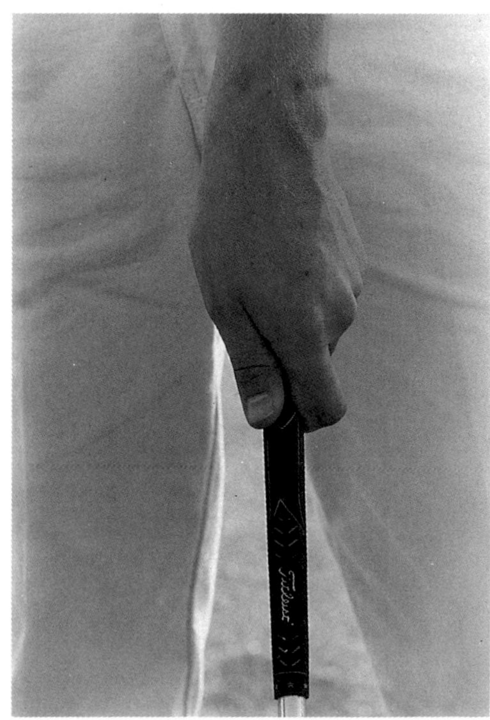

*If the handle lies too much in the palm of the hand (RIGHT), it is impossible to get the left hand around sufficiently to bring more than one knuckle joint into view, thus creating a weak grip.*

*By taking the handle too much into the fingers of the left hand (FAR RIGHT), the back of the hand is able to lie over the handle so that three or four knuckles are on view, thus creating a strong grip.*

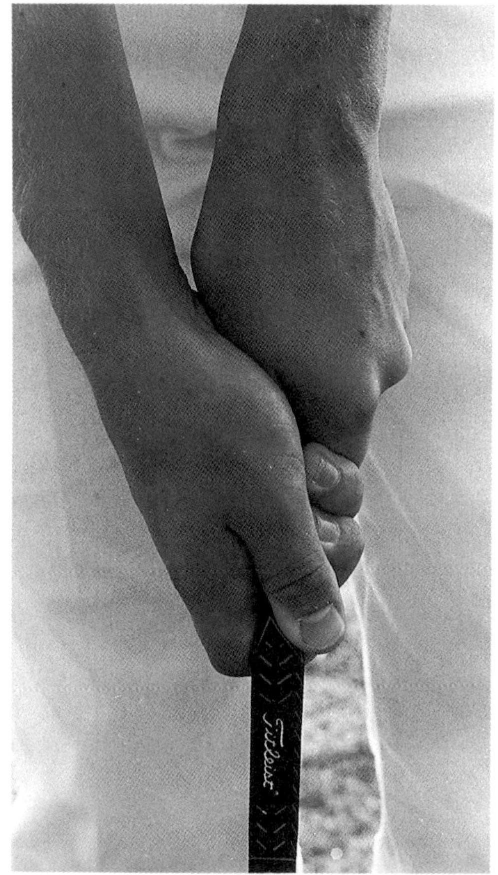

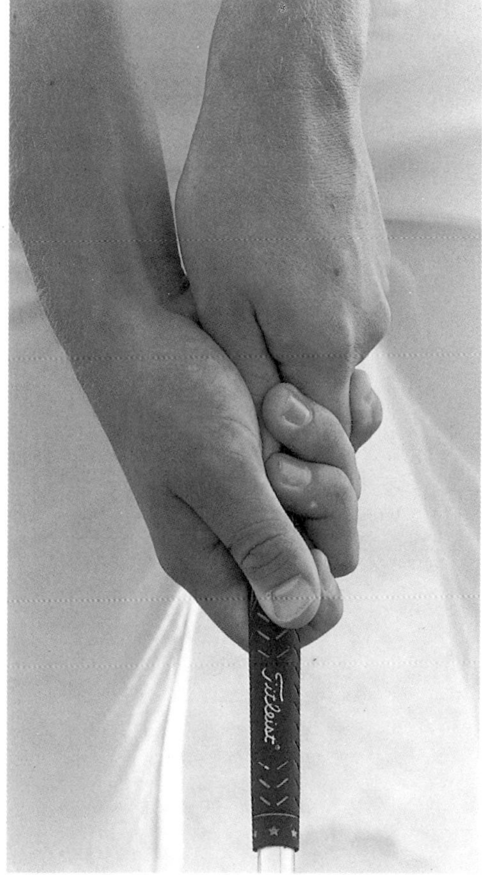

*The exact position of the left hand will determine how the right hand works. With the perfectly positioned left hand (FAR LEFT), it is easy for the right hand to be placed correctly on the handle. With the left hand in a weak position (BELOW LEFT), the right hand is able to climb over the left and the V shape formed points to the wrong shoulder. This is known as a weak grip. With the left hand in a strong position (LEFT), the right hand cannot get onto the handle but falls back under it. This is a strong grip.*

the left. This also happens – particularly with beginners – with a strong right hand. There is a great temptation to make the naturally stronger hand grip the club with the palm rather than the fingers. Having turned off to the right in the back swing, the right forearm reverses this movement in the through swing and consequently turns the club-face into a closed position.

You cannot pay too much attention to the grip – and to the work of each hand – to make sure that they are balanced and able to perform their individual tasks. Keep in the back of your mind the principle that the weaker the grip the more you are likely to push or slice the ball, while the stronger the grip the more chance there is of pulling or hooking it.

## Faults in the swing

Having checked on the most likely faults to occur in the set-up, you should then concentrate on those problems associated with the back swing and through swing which can occur even if you have managed to rectify any initial faults.

**Swing plane** Although mentioned again here as part of the fault-finding routine for the swing, many problems with the swing plane stem directly from the stance. It could well be that you have not lined your body up correctly or that you are standing too near or too far from the ball. Always bear in mind that ideally you should aim to maintain the same plane throughout the swing. This will help to insure that the line the club takes on the back swing will hopefully be as close to the line it continues to hold in the through swing as possible.

If the back swing is too flat, the club-

*If you adopt a flat swing plane, perhaps for a hook shot, you can see clearly how the head is twisted as the club travels flat around the body (RIGHT). Then, in the through swing, the exaggerated roll of the hands gives a clear indication that the follow-through will be very rounded.*

*Seen from above, use of the correct swing plane demonstrates how comfortably the club circles around the body according to its length (LEFT).*

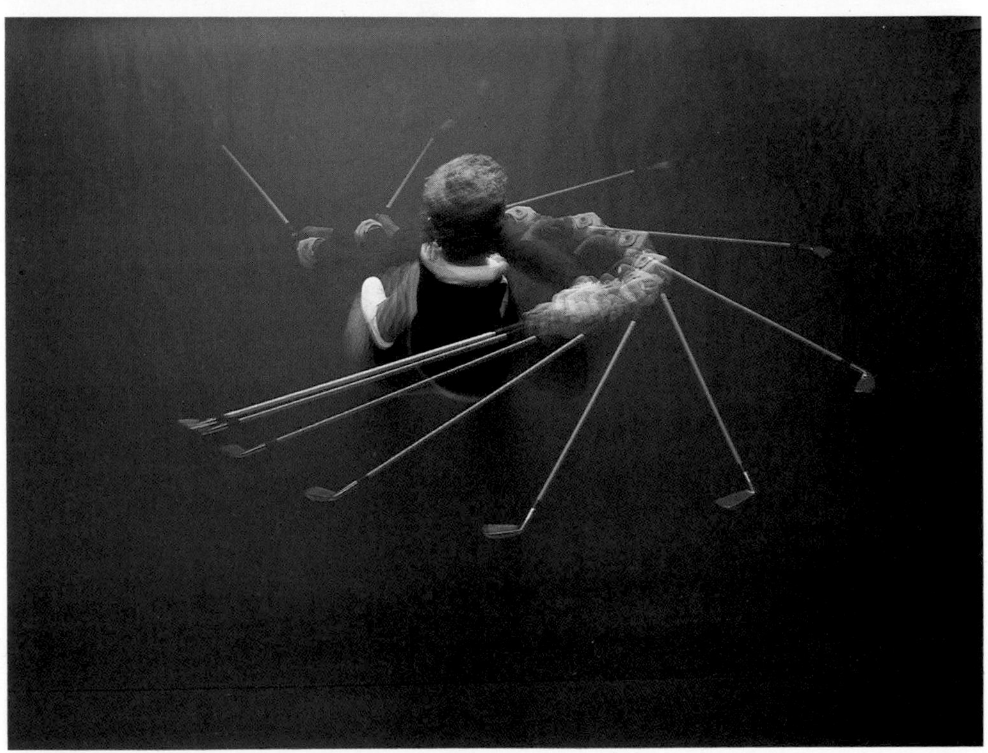

*The steep pick-up into the back swing, caused by an overly upright swing plane, results in a failure to turn fully at the top of the back swing. With the down swing the angle of attack is onto and across the ball, rather than back into it (LEFT).*

*This sequence illustrates the benefits of swinging the club on the correct plane to suit one's physique (RIGHT), where the shoulder turn is easily completed and the balance at the top of the back swing is obvious. With too upright a swing (TOP RIGHT), which is incorrect for the player's physique, the body turn has been limited and the club will now swing down across the ball. The damage done by the swing being too flat (BOTTOM RIGHT) is that the body is twisting rather than turning and the left heel has no chance of lifting off the turf. Movement is restricted and there is a dramatic loss of power in the swing.*

head will come down and through the ball from the inside of the target line. Unless you can square up the club-head, the ball will travel off to the right. If, on the other hand, the back swing is too steep and the turn of your shoulders is restricted, the club-head will probably come down in the through swing from the outside of the target line and move across and inside the ball. With the longest clubs, the woods, you will end up slicing, while with the short irons you will send the ball off to the left.

**Back swing** It is a great pity that, having perfected your grip, you should lose this advantage at the top of the back swing. But it can and does happen. This can be caused partly by overreaching, where

*It is very common when the swing is too flat (FAR LEFT) to find that the club cannot get anywhere near parallel to the ball-to-target line when it reaches the top of the back swing. This is described as being "laid off." Occasionally, when the left side of the body is allowed too much freedom in the back swing, the club can actually travel to a point where it lies "across the line" (LEFT).*

the hands are left to control the club after the shoulders and arms have gone as far as they can. Often in this situation they are unable to cope. This is one reason why it is so important to coordinate the various parts of the body involved in the swing, so that when you reach certain critical stages they are all functioning together and helping each other .

Control over the club at the top of the back swing can also be lost, of course, through poor gripping. Where the left hand grip is weak, the club tends to roll and the handle pushes against the fingers. In extreme cases these cannot cope with the extra pressure put on them and they lose control.

Ideally at the top of the back swing the club should end up in a line parallel to that of the target line. Sometimes it has not traveled far enough, which may be the case where a player has difficulty in achieving a full enough body turn. In this instance, extra movement can be achieved by lifting the left heel. However, the problem is more often caused because the shoulders were not set up in line with the shot in the first place, but were positioned slightly open, possibly because the ball was too far forward in the stance to begin with. The result in this case is that the amount of turn in the back swing is restricted and the club will adopt an out-to-in swing path.

Whatever the case, there is a great temptation not to make the necessary body adjustments and start the swing again, but to adjust the position of the

*When you reach the top of the back swing, great pressure is put on all the moving parts of the body. But that part under the greatest stress are the end fingers of the left hand. The difference between a controlled back swing (RIGHT) and an overly aggressive back swing (BELOW RIGHT)—where the fingers have been prized open—is clear to see. The exaggerated version of this fault is described as the "piccolo" grip.*

*The swing plane and swing path are closely related, as is demonstrated here. Where the swing plane is too flat (FAR LEFT), the club on the down swing will approach the ball on a swing path that is in-to-out (LEFT). Where the swing plane is too upright (BELOW FAR LEFT), the club on the down swing adopts a swing path across the ball from out-to-in (BELOW LEFT).*

club by misuse of the wrists.

By the same token, sometimes the club is swung too far around and is actually pointing in across the target line. The fault in this case may lie in the fact that the shoulders were closed in the stance and therefore came around too far in the back swing. Alternatively the problem may rest with the left hand, where the wrist has been cocked back too far. If this is not corrected, it will affect both the angle and direction of the through swing.

**Through swing** Many of the faults that become evident at this stage, especially at thc point of impact between the club-head and ball, will have emanated from earlier mistakes in the set-up or back swing. One particular problem that can occur during the down swing is hitting the ball too early. This is where the club-head reaches the ball ahead of the hands. Another, related problem, is hitting the ball too late, where the club-head arrives just after the hands. In the

*Although it is very difficult to achieve, the feeling on impact with the ball should be that the hands are still slightly ahead of the club (RIGHT) to insure the perfect contact (ABOVE).*

*The natural instinct is to help the club-head through on the down swing, encouraging it to reach the ball ahead of the hands (TOP LEFT). This results in the ball being contacted too early, producing a mishit (TOP RIGHT).*

*In the effort to have the hands forward in the strike (LEFT) — and occasionally when the swing is too flat — the ball is hit too late (ABOVE). This results in the ball being pushed away to the right of the target.*

*The ideal strike is when the club-head approaches the ball correctly from just a fraction inside the imaginary ball-to-target line (TOP). When the club-head approaches the ball too much from the inside (CENTER), the ball will be pushed off to the right unless hand action rotates the club-head, causing the ball to spin back to the left. When the club-head approaches the ball too much from the outside (BOTTOM), the ball will be smothered to the left, unless the club-face is kept open, in which case the ball will spin back to the right.*

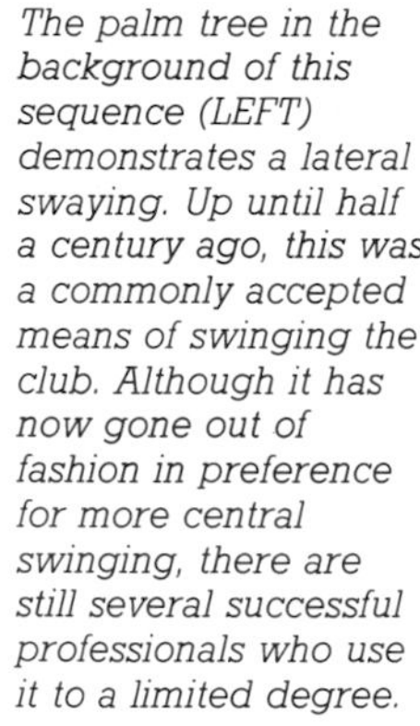

*The palm tree in the background of this sequence (LEFT) demonstrates a lateral swaying. Up until half a century ago, this was a commonly accepted means of swinging the club. Although it has now gone out of fashion in preference for more central swinging, there are still several successful professionals who use it to a limited degree.*

*Novice players often suffer from the problem of falling back (RIGHT, BELOW) because instinct tells them that they should help the ball upward into its flight. In fact, they should concentrate on driving the club forward (FAR RIGHT), as it is the loft on the club-face that takes the ball upward.*

first case, the ball will fly off to the left, while in the second the trailing club-head will force the ball off to the right.

The solution to these problems is timing – making sure that as the forearms move back into their original position on the down swing they coincide roughly with the moment the club-head makes contact with the ball. Likewise, there must be the right coordination between the top and bottom half of the body. If the top half moves back with the down swing before the hips and legs, then you will end up leaning into the shot. Alternatively, when too much of a lead is taken by the hips, the arms and shoulders trail and you will be left hanging back from the shot.

*Another unfortunate piece of advice commonly given is "keep your head down." Should the head be jammed down, then the result will be an incomplete follow-through. In addition, the hand action will become overactive as the club accelerates past the locked head position. The correct procedure is to strike through past your head (RIGHT), which in turn should come up with the natural flow of the swing so that you can enjoy watching the flight of the ball (FAR RIGHT).*

One controversial aspect of the through swing concerns what the head should be doing, particularly after the strike and into the follow-through. Traditionally it was always thought best for the head to be held fixed, looking downward, for as long as possible after the ball had been hit. However, nowadays, when the emphasis is very much on playing through the ball rather than at it, it is thought best to allow your eyes to follow the ball. This will, in turn, help you to achieve a full, flowing follow-through. This does not mean, however, that you should allow your head to move from its central position, since by moving the head you tend to move the shoulders as well. By all means allow your head to turn in the direction of the shot, but make sure you retain that angled position of the back to complete the swing plane.

The more serious problems arise if you move your head laterally during the swing. If you move it to the left as you strike, you will be inclined to hit outside the line of the shot: if you move it to the right in the back swing, you may sweep the club down inside the line and strike the turf before the ball. The point to remember is that, despite the movements in the rest of the body, the head should be held centrally and as still as possible throughout the shot. It is, in golf, the one part of the body that should not move – at least until after the ball has been sent on its way.

SECTION THREE

# USING THE CLUBS

The first basic steps in learning to play golf have been covered in detail in the previous section. While mastery of these elementary techniques is crucial if you are to become and remain a proficient player, there is still much to learn about the game of golf. Each shot you play demands a different approach and a particular type of club, depending on the circumstances. In a full set, this means a choice of 13 clubs until you are on the green. The other club, of course, is the putter, which is dealt with later. These clubs are divided into two main categories – woods and irons – and each has its own specific use during the course of a round.

## Woods

These are the first clubs you use on the course and are specifically designed for hitting the ball long distances. For this reason there is a much lower range of loft angles on the face of the woods than on that of the irons. However, it is important, particularly during the early stages of your golfing life, not to get carried away by the power of the woods and assume that they are there just to thrash the ball down the fairway as far as possible.

As with all the clubs, control is vital. Long shots will help you get to the green and play a significant part in returning a good score, but all the length in the world will be wasted if your ball lands in the rough, a hazard, or, even worse, out of bounds.

**Driver** This is the No. 1 wood which, if correctly used, will give you the maximum length of shot off the tee. Every player has this ultimate objective when teeing off, since a good drive down the fairway will reduce the distance to be covered with the next shot. At the shorter par four holes, it could get you close to the green and even on it.

With practice and the development of a sound technique, you should find teeing off one of the easier shots in the game. Remember that you do not have to worry about the lie of the ball or whether or not your club will dig itself into the ground. By using a tee peg, you can vary the height of the ball from the

*The perfect set-up when driving off the tee (RIGHT). The ball is positioned opposite a point just inside the left heel; the stance is at its widest — fractionally more than the width of the shoulders — and the hands are just slightly behind the ball.*

*One simple way of measuring how high the tee should be is to insure that the center of the ball is level with the top of the club-head. Here you can see how the height varies from a shallower-faced No. 3 wood to a deep-faced driver (LEFT).*

ground – and once confidence is gained you can tee the ball as high as 25mm (1in) off the turf. This enables you to gain maximum flight and distance by striking the ball slightly on the up, just after the base of the swing.

To achieve this, position the ball well forward in your stance and keep the club-head moving just slightly from inside the target line to outside, as it passes through the area of impact. Keep your weight just behind the ball and make sure that the desire for greater distance does not take you in front of it. It is important to have your left shoulder higher than the right. If you retain the correct posture through the strike, your left side should become firm while your right leg and right side bend as you come onto the toes of your right foot. To insure an upward contact on the ball, your hands should carry the club through and upward, taking it over your left shoulder so that it ends up almost resting diagonally across your shoulders at the finish of the follow-through.

*Since the nature of the driver would suggest that it sweeps the ball rather than punches it, you should have the impression of using a slightly flat swing plane — and certainly never an upright one (RIGHT).*

Striking the ball on the up is very important. If you do not have the ball positioned well forward and strike it at the base of the swing or fractionally earlier, you will probably do one of two things. Either you will drive the ball high into the air when contact is made high on the club-face, or you may smother it low along the ground. That is why you should start practicing with a fairly high tee peg to encourage yourself to sweep the ball away on the upswing.

As you master this technique and gain experience, there are situations where you might decide to have the tee peg higher or lower. With a low tee peg, the tendency when you strike down on the ball will be to slice it off to the right

*The value of having the club traveling to the ball with a slightly in-to-out swing path (which is the most powerful way of hitting a drive) is such that it pays to feel that the right shoulder and arm are lower than their partners at the set-up (LEFT). This also enables the ball to be struck slightly on the upswing.*

*The impression that the ball is hit on the upswing (ABOVE) is worth searching for, although in fact this does not take place. The best that can be achieved is for the club to travel level at the point of impact.*

*There is no joy in golf to match the feeling gained from a completed follow-through (RIGHT), while the ball soars on down the middle of the fairway. But this can only be achieved through a combination of balance and timing from a swing correctly in plane, as this sequence shows (ABOVE).*

slightly due to the loss of club-face loft. This is useful if there are hazards on the left-hand side of the fairway. With a higher tee peg, you will tend to hook the ball fractionally to the left, which will help you to avoid any hazards on the right-hand side of the fairway.

If you have trouble using your driver to tee off and cannot master the technique reasonably quickly, there is no harm in trying a No. 2 or No. 3 wood, although you may lose a little in length.

**Fairway woods** Again distance is the main reason for using woods on the fairway. Whether or not this is really practical will depend to some extent on the lie of the ball. If there is a reasonable amount of grass under the ball, then a fairway wood is relatively straightforward to use. Getting the right contact when the ball is lying tight to the ground requires much greater judgment and accuracy in the swing. The principles of playing with a fairway wood are basically the same – a full swing with a clean, smooth, sweeping action. As you play through the various woods, you will need to bring the ball back slightly in the stance from the forward position used for the driver.

One great advantage of a wood over an iron club when playing a ball in a tight lie is that the broader sole of the clubhead will tend to slide across the turf. With an iron, the tendency is to dig it into the ground, which causes the rhythm and momentum to be dissipated before you strike the ball. For this reason, if you are having trouble with, say, a No. 2 or a No. 3 iron, you would be better off playing that shot with a No. 4 or a No. 5 wood. This principle may also apply when playing the ball from the semirough. An iron may get caught up in the long grass because of the more downward, chopping action you adopt when playing the shot.

*By its very nature, the set-up position for each and every shot conveys a look that varies from aggression to delicacy. For a long drive (ABOVE) the hands reach out away from the thighs and the shoulders are forward to provide maximum power in the shot. As the club shortens through the middle irons (ABOVE RIGHT) to the pitching clubs (RIGHT), the hands come closer to the body and that previous look of aggression melts into one of finesse.*

*From the front view you can see clearly the correct attitude of the legs. With the wooden club (ABOVE LEFT) the stance is aggressive, then less so as you go down through the irons (LEFT) until you achieve the flexed position for the pitching clubs (ABOVE).*

## Irons

With the greater variation in degrees of loft, the range of irons in a set of clubs offers scope for extra height in the shot at the expense of length. You therefore require a greater degree of accuracy in the swing and the strike to effect the desired result in the shot. Precision striking is essential with irons, and a careful selection of club should eliminate any need to force the shot.

Irons do, however, offer more scope in the *type* of shot and are a very useful and necessary part of the golfer's armory. They can be broken down into three main groups – long, middle and short irons – not forgetting, of course, the specialist irons.

**Long irons** The ones most commonly used are the No. 2 and the No. 3 irons. What you have to bear in mind with these clubs is the fact that there is no real margin for error in the strike, which must be dead center on the club-face. This is in contrast to the woods where, even if you do make contact slightly off-center, you may still execute a reasonably well struck shot.

When compared with the woods, the strike for the irons should be more of a downward blow. However, when playing with a long iron you should still attempt more of a sweeping action. In other words, you should aim to clip the top of the grass on impact rather than punching down into the turf. How exactly you play the shot will depend on the lie of the ball.

Where the ball is sitting up reasonably well on the turf, you can aim to make contact with it fairly cleanly at the base of your swing. In this way you should be able to gain a fair amount of height in the shot. With a tighter lie, there is virtually no room for error and you will need a very accurate contact with the ball to obtain a clean strike. You will also need to have the ball positioned slightly further back in your stance than normal and aim to strike the turf and the ball in that order, creating a small divot. Of course, if the lie is too tight, then you may have to settle for using a more lofted club and losing some distance.

With the long irons, you will need to take up a slightly narrower stance than for the woods and keep the weight of your body just fractionally more to the left side. Since the club-head of the iron feels a bit lighter, there is a tendency to snatch at the ball to gain extra power in the shot. *This is fatal.* You will generate sufficient power in your shot through a good, smooth swing accelerating the club-head down into the strike and on into the follow-through.

A full shoulder turn is also very important, although you should make your back swing a little shorter than that used for woods. Provided you get the right rhythm into your swing, the club-head will do the required job for you.

**Middle irons** These are the Nos. 5, 6, and 7 irons. These clubs are generally the easiest to use because the swing is more compact and your whole action more positive.

With the shorter length of shaft becoming evident, you will be adopting a more upright stance, your feet will be closer together and the ball even further back toward the center of your stance. Although you will not be able to play a shot with this type of iron using a full sweeping action, you do not need to take too much of a divot out of the ground when striking down on the ball. Without restricting the shoulder turn, you should shorten the back swing down to about three-quarters of the full length of a drive and keep your weight more on the left side of your body.

With the extra loft on the club-face, you will gain more height and less distance with these irons. The increased back spin on the ball will help you check it from running on too far when landing, which makes these irons ideal for accurate shots to the green. However, you must be comfortably within range of the club you select so that you are not tempted to force the shot. When in doubt, use a slightly less lofted club to insure that you make the distance to your target.

When playing an approach shot with a middle iron, it is important to make sure you *do* get on the green, even if you leave yourself a longish putt to the hole. For this reason, it is often better to reduce the element of risk by playing to the widest part of the green.

You can use these irons for some chip-and-run shots when approaching the green, provided that the ground they have to run across is fairway grass. They can also be useful when playing over shorter distances into the wind, since they do not make the ball fly so high that the wind checks its progress. You can vary the length of the club by holding it down the handle and thus gain the advantage of low, controlled shots.

**Short irons** The Nos. 8 and 9 irons are the clubs to use when you are closer to the green – approximately 125m (140yd) or less away. Length here is not a problem and no great power is needed in the shot. What *is* essential is total accuracy. You should be aiming not just to get the ball on the green, but to place it in the optimum position – in other words, as close to the flag as possible.

With these clubs, you will be standing much closer to the ball, which should be central in your stance. The swing will be more upright and the club-head will drive down quite sharply onto the ball at the point of impact, creating a large divot before following through. Less swing is needed here. What is important is a smooth, firm down swing, continuing on into the through swing. Your weight should be looking forward onto the left side of the body as you strike through this type of shot.

The greater loft angle on these clubs will send the ball higher and, with the additional back spin, it should stop almost dead on landing. The temptation for beginners is to try to lift the ball into the air by hitting well under it. This is not necessary and should never be attempted. The loft of the club will do what is required, provided the contact with the ball is right.

One point that is worth remembering is that the club-head does not swing through quite straight on impact, because the down swing is slightly across the target line from out to in. If you do not make any adjustments in the stance, the ball may shoot off to the right. When playing a shot with the loftier clubs, therefore, you might need to aim your feet slightly to the left of the target, thus opening the stance fractionally. You will only achieve this through practice, but it will make a considerable difference to the accuracy and direction of your shots with the short irons.

*The angle of the shoulders at the set-up has a great bearing on the swing plane used. The high left side of the body when using the driver (ABOVE) will encourage the shallowest plane. As the angle drops through the middle irons (ABOVE RIGHT) and into the short clubs (RIGHT), the swing plane becomes more upright.*

*The effect of the shoulder line is clearly demonstrated when viewed from behind, with regard to a wooden club (ABOVE LEFT), a middle iron (LEFT) and a pitching wedge (ABOVE).*

## Specialist irons

These are the most lofted of all the clubs in the set and are designed to perform specific tasks on the course – although they may be used in other situations, particularly when playing past or out of trouble. Their individual functions are designated by their names – the pitching wedge and the sand iron.

*One of the secrets of good short iron play is that the swing must never be forced. It is far better to use a reduced back swing (BELOW) and gain full control of the through swing.*

**Pitching wedge** This club was originally adapted from the sand iron – the same club-face loft was retained but the head was made much lighter. It is now used as a general-purpose club for lifting the ball high into the air and dropping it almost vertically. For this reason it is invaluable near the green – anywhere within 96m (100yd) – since you can get enough length on the shot to carry it onto the green and at the same time stop the ball virtually dead where it lands.

To use this club, you need to stand in fairly close to the ball, with your feet positioned close to each other and the ball well back in the stance. As with the other short irons, you should reduce the length of the back swing and hit down on the ball. Because of the loft on the club, the ball will fly upward without any extra help from you, so do not be tempted to scoop the ball by using more hand movement or try to increase the power of the swing. Provided your swing technique is correct and you strike the ball accurately, the club will do the work for you.

The pitching wedge can also be useful when your ball is lying in fairly thick rough near the green. To play this kind of shot you must emphasize the chopping action, open the blade of the club slightly and grip further down the shaft. To avoid getting the club caught up in the long grass, aim directly down onto the ball and not just short of it. The loft angle will lift the ball clear of fairly heavy grass, even though you might be unable to gain any follow-through.

**Sand iron** Although this club is specifically designed for playing out of bunkers, it can also be used for shorter pitch shots to the green where maximum height and minimum distance are required – probably up to about 50m (55yd) from the target, provided the ball has a grassy lie. The techniques of playing the ball out of a bunker are discussed later (see page 170).

The main advantage to be gained by using this club near the green arises when there is an obstacle in the way of the shot that you need to clear. Due to the heavy back spin this club generates

*From a simple back swing, with its limited shoulder turn, you can make a much more direct, downward blow into the back of the ball (LEFT), which in turn will create more back spin.*

you will be able to stop the ball on the green very quickly.

Should you decide to use the sand iron with the closer and more straightforward shots, you should aim to brush the top of the grass or the ground quite lightly as you strike the ball, rather than hit down and into the ground slightly. Move your grip down the handle of the club and reduce the length of the back swing. You will need only minimal movement from your wrists in the swing. What movement there is should be encouraged in the legs and the arms, rather than in the hands.

You can, of course, use the sand iron for longer pitch shots, but it is important to remember that the striking technique in such cases should be the same as if you were using a pitching wedge. This means hitting down into the ball and making a divot just after contact.

*It is illegal to ground your club in a bunker prior to the down swing. Thus embedding your feet in the sand (BELOW) has a dual effect. Firstly it enables you to test the texture of the sand, and secondly it makes it easier for you to get the base of the down swing well below the level of the ball.*

*With the modern-day splash shot (RIGHT), the blade of the club does not make direct contact with the ball. Instead there is a cushion of sand between the two. Nevertheless, the hands and arms must continue on through the shot or else the club will be dragged to a sudden halt by the sand.*

## Putting

There have been numerous designs of putters over the years – even one with a shaft that entered the head vertically and allowed you to swing it between your legs, as if you were playing croquet. (This type, incidentally, has long since been outlawed.) Nowadays putters are generally upright, with the shaft entering the head at a slight angle.

Because of the type of club being used and the nature of the shot, the technique involved on the putting green is, of course, very different from that used on other parts of the course. Control is vital, since the shot needs to have exactly the right amount of pace and be deadly accurate. And, unlike any other shots on the course, the putt is played along the ground, which is why there is little or no angle of loft on the club-face.

As with any other shot on the golf course, however, working out the line of the shot and aiming correctly is all important and on these will depend where you take up your stance. However, it is possible to work on the basic techniques of the putting stroke without taking precise aim and these aspects are therefore being looked at first.

**Stance** You must make sure when you set up for the putt that you keep everything squarely in line with the direction of your aim, which as you will see later is not always directly to the hole. This means that your feet, which are only about six inches apart, hips, arms and shoulders must be lined up parallel to the target line. The body should be bent forward over the putter which, when the stroke is played, should be traveling in the same line as that of the ball toward the target. You should be able to move the putter backward and forward comfortably and smoothly, keeping it close to the ground at all times.

There is a tendency for learners to lean too far over the shot and this can be as bad as standing too upright. The effect of either of these two faults is to force the shoulders out of line when you apply the correct grip, with the left shoulder pointing off slightly to the left.

**Ball position** When preparing for the putt, you must make sure that the ball is positioned well forward in your stance. In fact, it should be roughly level with the inside of your left foot.

*The width of the stance when putting should never be more than 23cm (9in), and the ball should always be played from a point just opposite the left foot (RIGHT).*

*There can be no better advice on putting than to have everything square to the line of the shot. Common sense will tell you that if the shoulders, forearms, legs and feet are all parallel to the route along which the ball must travel, then it has to be easier to roll that ball truly toward the target. The standard, professional method of putting is well demonstrated here (LEFT). One very important feature is that the eyes are directly over the ball.*

**Grip** The grip used for putting is markedly different to that used for the other clubs. The handle should *not* cross the palm but rather pass just under the bottom of the left thumb, with the hand "laid off" so that the top of the handle is visible.

The left thumb should be on the top of the handle rather than to the side, and both this and the thumb of the right hand must point directly down the handle. With this arrangement you will insure that the left wrist stays well forward. The same rule as before applies when taking up the grip on the putter, with the handle placed in the left hand before adding the right.

*Since the putter is the one club in the bag that is used as near to the perpendicular as it is possible to get in golf, the grip changes from the traditional Vardon style to one where the thumbs are directly down the handle. The handle of the club passes comfortably up through the palm of the hands rather than in the fingers.*

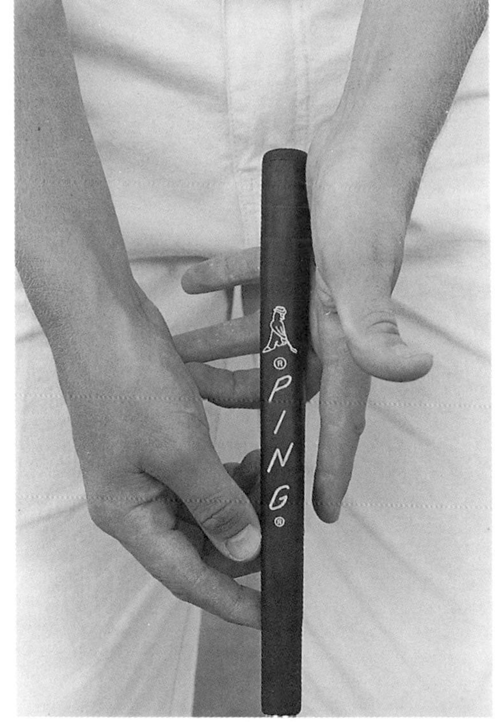


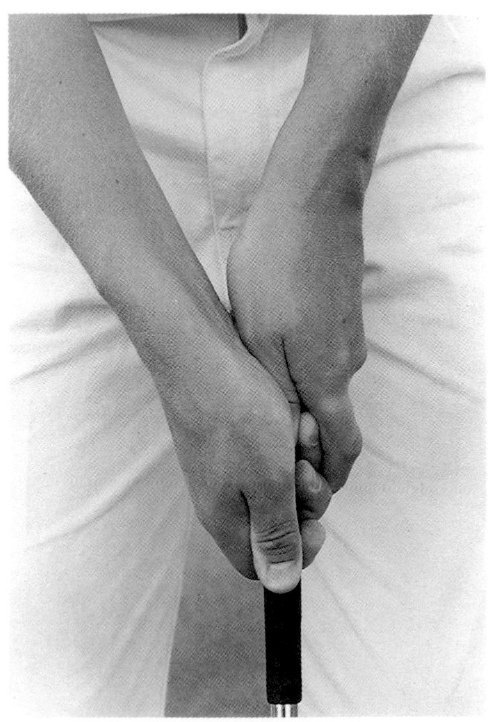

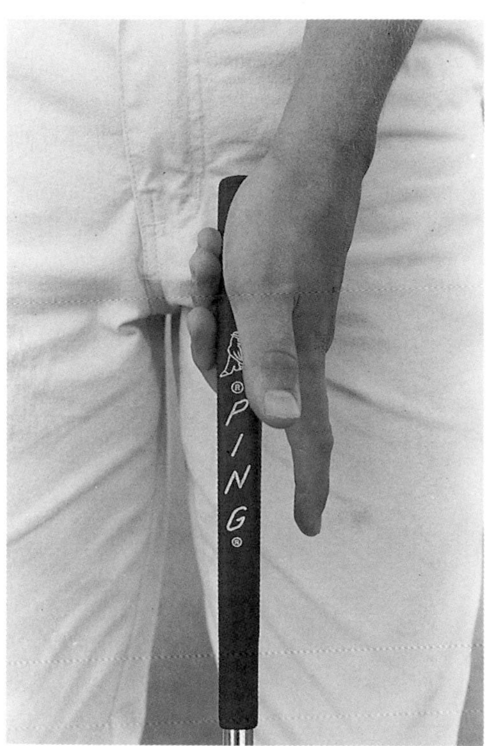


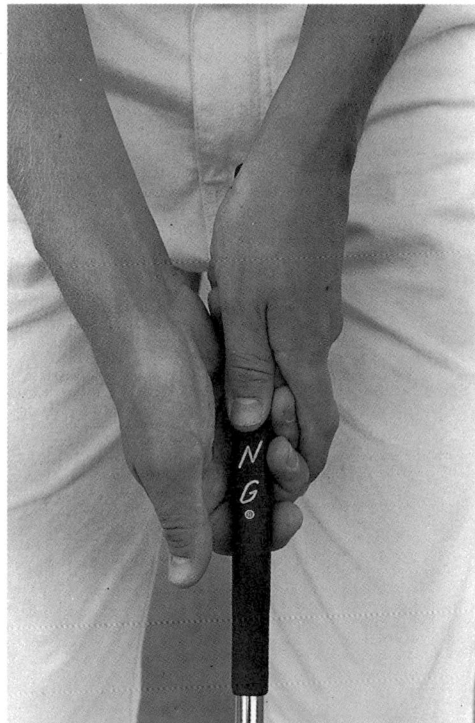

*Overlapping or interlocking are down to personal preference. Here a reverse overlap is used, where two fingers of the right hand are covered by the forefinger of the left.*

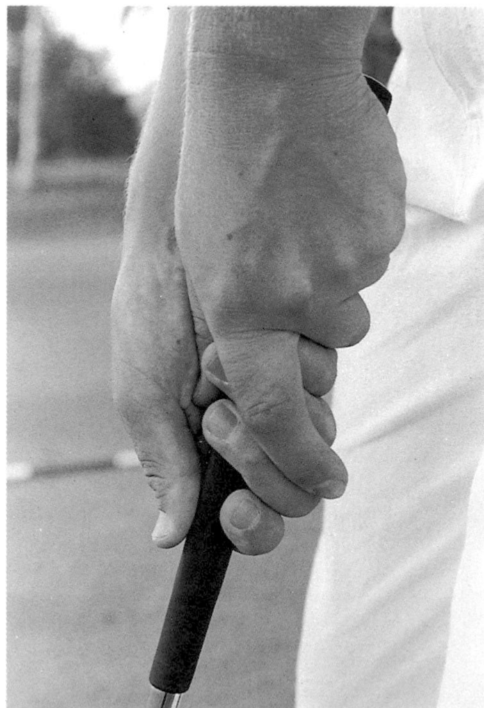

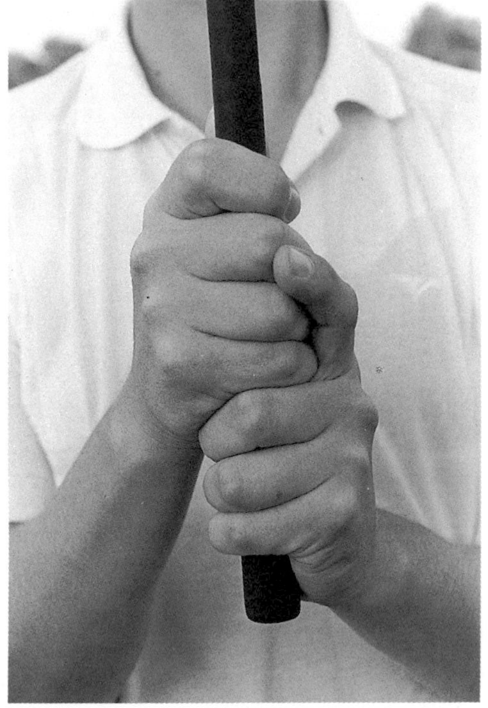

**The putt** Unlike all the other shots in golf, with the exception of the tiny chip-and-run shots, there should be minimal movement of the body when striking the ball on the green. Apart from the gentle to and fro swing of the arms and a slight rocking movement of the shoulders, the rest of your body should remain perfectly still – and particularly your head. Obviously you will move this in order to look up and down the line of the shot prior to hitting the ball, but once you are satisfied with your aim and have decided what strength to put into the stroke, your head should come down to look at the ball and remain there until well after you have stroked the ball towards the hole.

How you apply pace to the ball is, to a large extent, a matter of personal taste. There are two methods you can adopt. One is to maintain the same length of stroke (the total distance the putter travels back then forth along the target line) whether it is a short putt you are playing or a long one. The extra pace is applied by striking the ball harder.

The second method is to maintain a standard tempo throughout the putting stroke, regardless of the length of shot required. Players who prefer to do this then lengthen the stroke accordingly for the longer putts (by drawing the putter back then sending it further through) and similarly reduce it for the shorter putts.

*The nature of the putting grip tends to stifle wrist action rather than encourage it and this is ideal for the putting stroke, which comes more from a forearm and hand motion rather than a wrist and hand action (RIGHT).*

*One of the secrets of successful putting is to take the putter head back and through the ball with as smooth, short and low to the ground a movement as possible, as shown here from a front and side view (LEFT, BELOW).*

*Since it is almost impossible to find a putting green that is flat—not that any would be designed that way—it is necessary to learn how to "read" the green (RIGHT). The rolling ball will be affected by gravity and will therefore turn from the high side to the low side of any slope. Judging how high to the right or left to send the ball is known as "taking the borrow," a key factor in successful putting.*

The "plumb-bob" method (ABOVE) is a means of using the putter to gauge how much the ground slopes away from the vertical hang of the club. By lining up the lower part of the shaft through the ball and then bringing your eye up the shaft until it is level with the hole, however much the hole is to the right or left, that is the amount you should borrow when playing the putt.

*A tiny putt (LEFT) still counts as much as a massive drive, and it can prove very costly should one careless moment where concentration lapses be allowed to creep in . . .*

## Lining up the putt

Apart from adopting the right putting technique, it is also crucial to the success of the shot that you can line up the putt accurately by deciding how the green slopes and therefore where to aim the ball. Unfortunately it is rarely as simple as just aiming for the flag. Aspects that should always be given careful consideration include the grass itself – whether, for example, it is thick or close-cut, fine or coarse, damp or dry. Also relevant is how the green itself runs, whether it slopes up or down, or equally off to left or the right.

Since there can be no margin for error if you are attempting to hole out in as few putts as possible, you must also take into account the natural elements – and, in particular, the strength and direction of any wind that is blowing on the green.

Incidentally, before you get down on your hands and knees and start pulling the turf about, you should remember that testing the green itself is against the rules – even with a club-head. So all your investigations must be carried out with the eyes alone.

Needless to say, the drier and closer-cut the green, the faster the ball will run across it. Conversely, the damper and thicker it is, the slower the ball will travel. The stronger you play the shot, therefore, the less likely it is to be affected by the surface of the green — over reasonably short distances, at any rate.

**Sloping greens** The trouble with any slope, of course, is that if you play the ball along the ground it will be carried with the slope. If you do not make any adjustment when lining up the shot, the ball will fall agonizingly away from the target line instead of running straight to the hole. To compensate for this, you must therefore aim your putt up the slope first at just the right spot and pace so that the ball will then run down with the slope into or close to the hole. This is known as "taking the borrow."

Working out how much a green slopes and, therefore, where exactly to aim the ball so as to bring it back to the hole is not the easiest of tasks on the golf course. Those with a very good eye and an uncanny knack of judgment may be able to get it right most of the time. But

*On a sloping green (BELOW) it is essential that you allow enough for the slope and aim the putt so that the ball runs back down with the slope—hopefully into the hole. In such a situation much will depend on your judgment and plenty of practice.*

there is no doubt that this skill is somewhat of a gift not granted to every golfer. Fortunately, however, there is a method by which you can calculate fairly accurately the degree of the slope relatively easily and therefore where roughly to aim your ball.

Sometimes called the "plumb-bob" method, it works on a similar principle to that of the piece of equipment used to establish a true vertical. In the case of golf, the equipment used is the putter. The exercise is best carried out from a crouching position a pace or two from the ball. If this is a problem, then move further back and try it from the upright position. You must take up your position behind the ball so that it is in the line of sight between you and the flag. Then suspend your putter by holding it lightly near the top of the handle, so that the shaft appears to be directly over the center of the ball. Make sure you hold the putter so that its head is pointing either toward you or the hole. If not, the shaft will hang at an angle.

Take your eyes up the shaft to the point where it is level with the hole. In the case of a perfectly straight putt, where the ground is not sloping, the shaft will run right through the hole. But if the ground does slope, then this point will be either to the right or to the left of the hole and it is to this point that you should aim your shot.

While this method is quite useful and does offer a reasonable guide, it cannot of course tell you *how much* the green slopes up or down toward the hole or about the condition of the turf. These factors are all relevant in assessing what pace you need to play the shot.

Where the green runs downhill to the hole as well as sloping to one side, you should take the precaution of increasing the amount of the borrow – that is, aiming to a point even wider than the one indicated by the plumb-bob method. Conversely, where the green runs uphill, you should aim somewhere between the estimated point and the hole.

At the end of the day, working out the slope and other relevant conditions on the green will depend on your experience. The more practice you have play-

*When putting down and across a split-level green (BELOW), you must take into account the amount the ball will accelerate down the slope and how this will affect the direction of the ball as it crosses the down slope. Once you have chosen the point at the top of slope through which the ball must pass, concentrate on this and try not to think of the hole itself.*

ing on different types of green, the more proficient you will be at judging the composition of a green and playing it accurately.

**Adverse weather** Unfortunately slopes are not the only problem you are likely to encounter when you get to the green. Rain can make quite a difference to the run of the ball, since the wet grass will take much of the pace out of the shot. In this case, you will need to reduce the amount of borrow to compensate since you will have to play a stronger shot.

Strong winds can also play havoc with your calculations, and any allowances you make will depend on whether the wind is blowing down the slope or up it. Where it is with the slope, you will have to increase the borrow, while with the wind blowing against the slope, the effect will be greatly reduced and you will therefore need to allow much less borrow.

**Split-level greens** Sloping greens pose one set of problems which you will, with experience, overcome, but further problems await you in the shape of split-level greens. The secret of playing on this type of green is to have a good look at both sections. Check on the slope between each section and get firmly fixed in your mind a marker spot to which and through which you should aim the ball. (Naturally you will have to check as to whether either level of green slopes and take this into account as previously described.)

The easier approach to this type of green is definitely from the lower level up to the higher level. There are several reasons for this. For a start, you should be playing a firmer putt to get the ball up the hill. Also, because the higher section of the green will be nearer to your own eye level, you will find it a lot easier to check the lie of the turf and where the slope may be.

In this situation, you need to fix only one marker point, at the top of the slope on the edge of the higher level. This is because the strength of the shot needed to carry the ball up the hill should, in normal cases, override any problems in the lower level turf. Thus you can concentrate on establishing the correct spot on the top level from which your ball will hopefully run to the hole.

Putting down from the higher level to the lower one is more problematical, since you will not be able to use so much strength in the shot. You must also take into account the conditions of the turf on both levels, particularly since the ball will gain added pace from the steepness of the down slope. It is essential to judge what the ball's reaction will be, both in pace and direction, and estimate the point at which it must roll over the top of the slope. That is the place you must aim for and it should take your mind off the hole itself.

The biggest problem with downhill putts is judging the pace of the shot. If you underhit the ball, it might not even make the slope and you are then faced with a similar problem all over again. Equally, if you hit the shot too hard, the ball will pick up extra pace down the slope and run well past the hole. But, whatever you do, make sure the ball gets onto the lower level, even if it is not as close as you would wish to the hole.

Where to look when playing this type of putt is equally crucial. One thing you must not do is be tempted to look at the hole. Having worked out your marker point, concentrate just on this. Go for the marker point and trust your judgment.

Life will be made even more complicated if you have to play up or down a split-level green at an angle. Coping with this is basically a matter of experience. The general rule, however, is to overestimate the borrow you need and make sure, if you are putting up the slope, that you get the ball onto the higher level. Letting the ball roll back down the hill can prove disastrous.

## Faults in the shot

Having spent some time trying to master the basic techniques of golf, setting up correctly for the shot and swinging the club accurately, you will understandably be eager to get out on the course to put what you have learned into practice. While this is, of course, part of the learning process, you must take care not to waste the experience by becoming preoccupied with playing the holes at the expense of your technique. Sadly, this does happen all too often, and you will probably only know when your technique has gone awry after you have struck the ball. It is important at this stage not to let things get you down. Golf is a game that requires patience as well as skill, and if you become unduly depressed by your early performance you will find it even harder to make real progress.

The fact that you *do* go wrong is not nearly as important as being able to analyze *where* you went wrong and to take the necessary steps to rectify the problem. If you can do this, then each time you play a similar shot you can remind yourself of what happened the last time. This will enable you gradually to iron out most, if not all, of those faults. Not only will this make for more enjoyable golf, but it should also be more successful, too. The following are some of the most common problems you are likely to encounter when playing a shot – study them carefully and keep a look out for any symptoms in your own technique.

**Ballooning** This is one of the first faults you are likely to encounter occurring as it does with the tee shot, where the ball is perched off the ground on a tee peg. The fault comes about when contact is made with the very bottom of the ball and very much with the upper part of the club-face. Instead of a good firm drive from the meat of the club-face, the effect

*If you fail to maintain a central position, your down swing will be narrowed and the club-head will be brought downward to the ball (TOP). As a result most of the ball will pass over the top of the club (ABOVE), ripping the paint as it does so and ballooning up into the sky.*

*Efforts to artificially cause the ball to lift quickly can result in the club-head being brought into the ball too soon, so that it catches the turf first (LEFT). This is known as fluffing the shot.*

of ballooning is to send the ball soaring upward with violent back spin hardly any distance down the fairway.

Check first on the club you are using. You could be playing with a driver that has insufficient loft for your standard of play. Or the problem may lie in the fact that you are using one of the more lofted woods while having the ball teed too high. The tell-tale sign is usually a severe scuffing of the paintwork on the top of your club.

Apart from using the wrong type of club, the areas to check are the hands and the shoulders. A contributory factor in the grip will be whether your right hand is holding the club-handle in the palm and not with the fingers. Although with this type of grip you will get a greater feeling of strength, the tendency is for the hand to turn the club-face in and narrow the down swing, crushing the ball rather than playing it with a sweeping action.

Another reason for ballooning the ball is bringing the club down in the through swing at too steep an angle, caused by not turning your shoulders enough in the back swing. By readjusting your grip and making sure, from a square stance, that you bring your shoulders back the full 90 degrees and gain the impression of swinging from in to out through the ball, you should enjoy much longer, less lofted, driving from the tee.

**Fluffing** This describes very accurately what happens when the club-head hits the ground before striking the ball. In extreme cases, of course, the effect will be to see the ball trickle forward a short distance, since all the impetus has been taken out of the shot.

This problem is exaggerated when using the loftier clubs, since with these you are bringing the club down on a much steeper swing plane and thus the deeper into the ground the club-head is likely to sink. At the other end of the range, the woods should be traveling on a much shallower plane and therefore even hitting the ground first may not unduly affect the strength with which the ball is struck.

Fluffing tends to come about because the right hand turns over the left in the through swing before the club-head has struck the ball. The culprit here can be the left hand and the fault was probably committed 'way back at the time you set

*Topping is one of the beginner's common faults, although it can also happen to more experienced players should an element of anxiety creep into their play. Tension can reduce the length of the arm, in turn raising the club-head so that it strikes well up on the surface of the ball (RIGHT).*

up for the shot and adopted the grip.

One of the reasons why, at the set-up, you should bring the club forward to the left hand and not move this hand back to grip the club is just this. With a more angled left wrist, there is more of a flick movement in the through swing and this encourages the right hand to go over the left too early. The result is that you hit the ground before the ball. The policy should be "hands forward at the address, then swing through the ball and not at it."

**Topping** As the term implies, this occurs when you hit over the top of the ball, often because you have not swung the club through at its full length. Another reason may be that you are concentrating on the top of the ball so much that you end up hitting that part of the ball rather than below its center. The same problem will occur if you lift your head too soon and therefore raise the base of the swing off the ground.

A large part of the cause of topping can be traced to a lack of confidence and a failure to relax sufficiently in the shot. This can cause your muscles to tighten up just enough to alter the length of the swing. Topping the ball does not necessarily imply that there is a basic fault in your technique, and there is no obvious and simple way of solving this problem. All you can hope to do is put in as much practice as possible – and certainly try one or two practice swings before you step up to strike the ball.

The best exercise is to stand with the base of the club-head just touching the grass. Move it backward and forward using a part swing and then build this up to a full swing. All the time you should be able to hear the club brushing over the top of the grass. Having established this length of swing, you should hopefully stop topping the ball.

*Toeing (TOP) occurs when the club-head is brought down on the ball as the right hand passes the left too early in the down swing. One way to cure this is by swinging through the ball more positively.*

*Shanking (ABOVE) occurs when the swing path toward the ball is too much from in to out, probably caused by swing back from the ball on too flat a swing plane.*

**Toeing** This is an extreme version of slicing (see Index). It occurs when the ball is struck with the toe end of the club-face and inevitably shoots off to the right.

There are several causes of toeing. One of the most elementary faults is to take up your stance too far away from the ball. This causes you to swing inside the ball and any contact made will be with the very end of the club-head. Equally you may be hitting the ball too early, with your right hand coming over the left before the point of impact and therefore turning the club-face before it makes contact with the ball. In this case, you will probably fluff the shot as well.

To rectify the problem, check just how far you are standing from the ball and move in a fraction if necessary. Also, look at the line of your stance. If your feet are aligned to the right, so that the stance is slightly closed, you may find yourself hitting at the ball too early. In this situation you are forced to make an adjustment with your right hand in an attempt to hit the ball straight and not off to the right, as would otherwise be the case.

**Shanking** This can prove to be the most violent form of mishit. By striking the ball with the neck of the club rather than the face, the ball will normally shoot off to the right, often at almost 90 degrees to the target.

The reason this happens is because you are standing too far away from the ball and your swing plane is too flat. Thus, as the club-head travels down on a path moving from inside the line of the shot, across the face of the ball and on the outside of the line, the neck of the club catches the ball on the inside.

Although the natural reaction is to move back a little so you are standing even further from the ball, this will prove even more disastrous, since you will have flattened your swing even more. You need to do quite the opposite. Move in closer to the ball and make sure it is positioned slightly further forward in the stance. From this more upright position, your swing plane will be steeper. With accurate swinging – and the club-face turned fractionally open – you should now hit the ball cleanly with the face of the club and not the neck.

Faults are all part of learning the game of golf and even the best players have problems from time to time. Although you are never going to eliminate them completely, you should learn the reasons why they occur and how to cure them. Home-made remedies may work occasionally, but it is far better to tackle the basic problems and so reduce the chances of such faults becoming features of your game.

SECTION FOUR

# PLAYING THE COURSE

The basic techniques so far discussed are intended to enable you to play the ball straight at a height and distance determined to an extent by the type of club you are using. Having gained experience and reached a reasonable level of proficiency, you may start to believe that you have mastered the art of golf and can confidently go out and play around any course.

Unfortunately it is not quite that simple – and if it were, people would very soon tire of the sport and give up through boredom. What makes golf a fascinating game is the fact that it involves a great deal of variety with every single shot. This is because the courses are designed in such a way that each hole offers a new challenge, a different problem and a changing situation.

Although you may have learned to master the basics – aiming, setting-up and swinging – the challenge of the game has only just started. You have still to learn how to control the ball and send it just where you want – and this involves the use of spin. You must learn how to adapt your stance and your swing when playing the ball on a slope and, equally, you must be able to play the ball out of the bunker you will inevitably find yourself in from time to time.

Then there is the problem of the weather. Although you may be used to watching golf with a background of clear blue skies and sun-drenched fairways, life on the course is rarely as idyllic as that. Depending on where you play, the hazards of wind and rain will need to be confronted. In such conditions, you have to adapt your standard game if you are to survive and cope successfully.

## Playing with spin

In an ideal world the golf club would travel true into the back of every ball and the loft, according to the club being used, would impart only one kind of spin – back spin. The ball would travel directly on target, soaring to the appropriate height and landing dead on target.

However, golfers are not machines and golf courses are uneven places exposed to all sorts of conditions, and almost every shot played on them is an original one. Therefore another type of spin is created, whether out of choice or by accident, often violent in its extent. It is called side spin.

Moving a ball so that it turns off its original course can, when done accidentally, be soul-destroying. But when it is applied intentionally it is a most rewarding and stroke-saving ability. There is, therefore, a great advantage to be had in possessing the skill that can turn a ball in flight. You can fight the wind or choose to use it, and you can avoid hazards or curve the ball around them.

The two basic types that golfers use are back spin and side spin. The first is the easier and more obvious to apply, since by striking the ball accurately and cleanly the job is done. Because of the way club-faces are angled, particularly the more lofted ones, and the fact that the best place to strike the ball is just below center, you have already achieved your objective.

Although the height given by back spin does not alter the direction of the ball, the effect it has when the ball lands is invaluable. On impact with the ground, the ball should either stop dead or, depending on the amount of spin applied, roll back a short way. This type of control can be crucial. Side spin is a lot harder to apply, since you have to not only alter the swing path of the club but also to strike the ball with the club-face off square.

Side spin takes one of two forms. Either you can hit the ball off to the left in such a way that as the spin takes effect the ball comes back into line, or you can hit it off to the right and then bring it back in from that direction. The first type of spin, depending on how great an arc you send the ball along the shot, is described as drifting from a "fade" to a "slice" in extreme cases. When playing the ball out to the right with gentle spin this is described as a "draw" shot, while with extreme spin the shot is a "hook."

**Back spin** The timing and accuracy of your swing direction is crucial to the imparting of back spin. As already mentioned, because of the degree of loft built in to the face of the clubs, you only have to hit the ball cleanly and squarely with a lofted club to impart back spin. Obviously, the more lofted the club, the greater the back spin. So, whereas with the No. 1 iron you will get maximum distance for an iron shot but minimum lift and spin, with the loftiest iron – the sand iron – you will achieve maximum height and spin, but little distance.

However, there is a further way of increasing the back spin on the ball, which you will need to master if you want this type of control on longer shots where you will be using clubs with less loft. It involves delaying the uncocking of the wrists until very late in the down swing so that the ball is struck with a more descending blow. The base of the swing is moved beyond the ball so that your club-head strikes the ball and then, after an inch or so, the ground. You can also achieve this by putting more of your weight onto the left side of your body as you swing down. This is a fairly advanced skill, which is used by experienced players, and it is better not to attempt it until you are very confident.

There are obviously times when you will not want so much back spin on the ball. The most common situation is from the tee, when normally you want your

*Golf is rarely a straightforward game, and it is therefore essential to understand how to play a variety of spin shots in order to avoid trouble—or at least extricate yourself from it when necessary (RIGHT).*

drive to run on as far as possible. Fortunately there is no real problem here, since the driver has a minimum degree of loft in the club-head.

Choosing a club with less loft is, in fact, the simplest method of reducing back spin. When using a club with less loft than normal, move your grip down the club-handle so that you are holding the club as though it were a shorter, more lofted pitching club. Then position yourself so that the ball is slightly further back in the stance than it should be for the type of club you are using. There will be occasions when you may decide to use this technique to insure plenty of run on the ball.

There is another way of emphasizing the reduction of back spin on the ball, and that is to keep the movement of your hands and wrists to a minimum during the through swing, since activity in this area always encourages spin on the ball.

*The spin everyone searches for initially is back spin, which is the true spin of a ball struck directly from a perfect swing plane and on an accurate swing path (RIGHT, FAR RIGHT). The result is that the control put on the ball can bring it to a very abrupt halt when it lands.*

*One problem when a ball with back spin lands (ABOVE) is that it can leave a nasty pitchmark, which should be repaired. But this mark is the sign of quality in the strike. The fact that the ball was still turning quite violently backward when it struck the ground shows how effective the contact of the blade of the club on the ball was in the first place.*

*In order to turn the ball in the air from left to right, it is essential that the club travels through the ball from outside to in (RIGHT), bearing in mind that the face of the club should be kept open from that swing path.*

**Side spin** The determining factor in applying side spin to the ball so that during its flight it alters direction – either to the left or the right – is the way the club-head faces on impact with the ball. When the club-head is open (or angled back) the ball will travel off in a straight line and then veer to the right. This is known as a slice spin shot. When the club-head is closed (or angled forward), the opposite will occur, where the ball starts straight and then moves off to the left. This is known as a hook spin shot.

Imagine the situation where you are hitting toward a target with what is known as a direct swing path. With the club-head open, the ball will start traveling toward the target, then veer off to the right. Equally, with the club-head closed the ball will start straight then move off to the left.

So how, when you apply spin to the ball, should you play the shot to insure that when the ball moves to the left or right in flight it will eventually return on line with the target? The answer is to send it off in a different direction to begin with, and to do this you need to alter the direction of the swing path.

At this stage you may well feel totally confused but in fact the principle is quite straightforward. To simplify the situation think in terms of three sets of shots. The first is where your swing path is directly towards the target; the second is where your swing path travels from inside the target line to outside; and the third is where your swing path travels from outside the target line to inside.

The effect of an open or closed club-head when playing with a direct swing path has already been discussed. When you change the direction of the swing path similar principles apply.

If you have a swing path that travels from inside to outside the target line, when the club-head is also square to that direction at the point of impact, the ball will travel off to the right in a straight line and not deviate. Where the club-head is open from that swing path on impact, the ball will travel off to the right then veer even further to the right. With

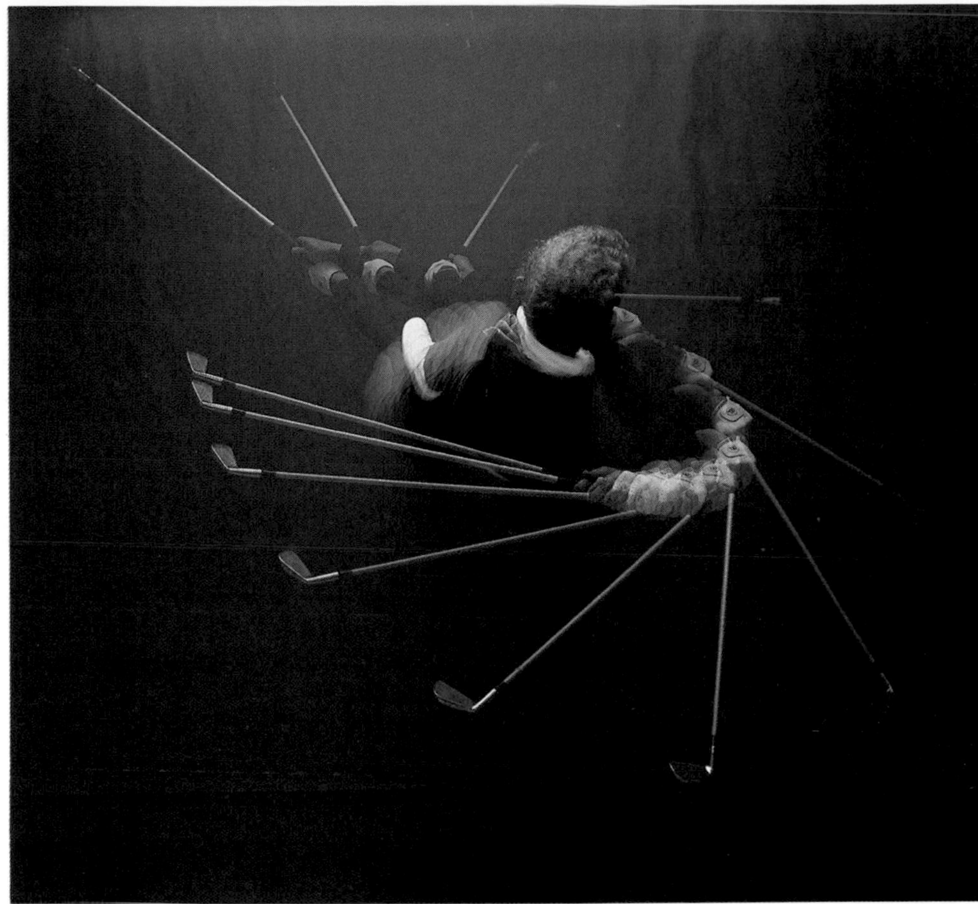

*In order to apply hook spin to the ball, moving it from right to left in the air, the swing path must be such as to deliver the club-head to the ball traveling from in to out across the ball-to-target line (LEFT), with the club-face closed from that swing path.*

the club-head closed, it will move off to the right then veer back to the left.

If your swing path is from outside the target line to inside it, when the club-head is square to that swing path at the point of impact, the ball will travel off to the left in a straight line and keep going. Where the club-head is open on impact, the ball will travel off to the left then curve back to the right. With the club-head closed on impact, the ball will go off to the left and then veer sharply away even further left.

How far off target to the right or the left you play the shot will depend on how much you alter your swing path – from inside to outside or vice-versa. Likewise, the amount the ball deviates when in flight will depend on how much you angle the club-head open or closed from the chosen swing path.

Thus far the principles of side spin have been discussed – what actually needs to happen to the ball to send it in different directions. Having understood how side spin works, you will need to learn how to apply it.

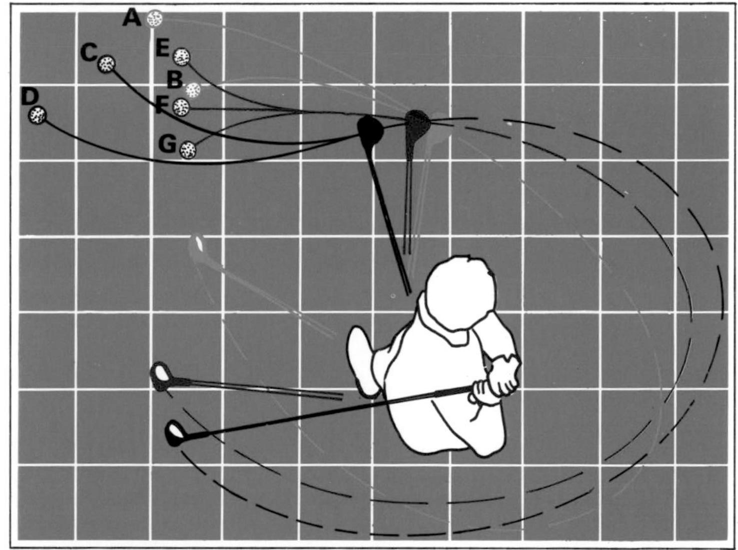


*Side spin (ABOVE) is created by a combination of club-head angle and swing path direction. An in-to-out swing path with a closed club-head produces a "draw" (A) or, in extreme cases, a "hook" (B). An out-to-in swing path with an open club-head produces a "fade" (D) or, in extreme cases, a "slice" (C). A direct swing path with a square club-head produces a straight shot (F), with the club-head open it produces a slight "fade" (E), and with the club-head closed a "draw" (G).*

## Applying slice spin

Here you need to select the less lofted clubs in the set. The driver is suitable, as is the No.3 wood and probably any iron up to a No.5. The difference in the stance for a hook spin and a slice spin shot is that with the latter you do need to alter the complete stance.

The stance for a slice spin shot should be open from the target line, with feet and hips turned to the left along with the shoulders. Make sure that the ball is further forward in the stance than usual and keep the club-head facing the target, which means it will appear open from the swing path you require for the shot.

When you swing back, you will find that there is nowhere near the same amount of turn in the shoulders and that your swing plane is much more upright, enabling the club to travel down and through the ball from the outside of the target line to the inside.

Again you must make sure that the club-head makes contact with the ball as it crosses the target line. Because the club-head is open on impact with the ball, it will create a clockwise rotation that will eventually take the ball off to the right of its original direction.

*One way of getting past an obstacle such as this tree (RIGHT) is to slice around it. This can be done by using a straight-faced club and swinging with an upright swing plane so that the swing path is from out to in, while the blade is kept open long into the follow-through.*

## Applying hook spin

You need to select a lofted club when attempting to play with hook spin, keeping your left hand forward in the stance and angling the club back slightly. The ball should be positioned further back in the stance than normal for the club you are using.

You may be tempted to close the stance somewhat, by turning your body across the target line. However, the only part of your body that should be turned in to the right is your shoulders, since the line of your shoulders – as with the normal direct line of the swing – will determine the line your swing path takes. In the case of hook spin, this needs to be inside to outside across the target line. How far to the right you need to close your shoulders will depend on how far off line you want to send the ball initially.

You will find from this stance and adjusted posture that the swing plane gets shallower and your body turns much more. When you bring the club down, this helps to insure that it crosses the target line as the ball is struck. Because the club-head is closed when it makes contact, this will create an anti-clockwise rotation of the ball that will eventually take it off to the left of the original direction of the shot. The more spin you want to put on the ball, the more you need to exaggerate the changes you make to the normal techniques.

*It takes a great deal of courage, once you have aimed sufficiently right of an obstacle such as these trees (RIGHT), to then create an in-to-out swing path, for the impression gained is that the ball will be sent even further to the right than is required. However, with skill and practice, the club-face will be closed from the swing path at the point of impact, causing the ball to turn quite violently in the air from right to left.*

## When to use spin

The obvious advantage to be gained by using spin is when you need to bend the ball around an obstacle on the course that stands between you and the target. However, many professionals also use spin to advantage in normal shots because they feel they have a greater control over the ball and know that it can only travel in a specific direction, depending on the type of spin they apply. This is not a use recommended for the beginner.

Hook spin is useful when there are problems on the right-hand side of the fairway. Possibly it is an awkward tree, which you are unable to lift the ball over, or maybe a hazard such as water, a bunker or an "out of bounds" area. Those players confident of gaining sufficient length and height with the ball to surmount such hazards may go for the straight shot. The choice facing the less committed player is either to play safe by hitting away from the trouble or to use spin to play around it.

Slice spin can be of particular advantage once you have understood its effects and mastered the control of it. Whereas a straight shot, slightly mishit, could end up to the left or right of the target, with slice spin you know that the ball will move to the right and should be able to judge how far it will do so.

The higher up the ball's surface your club makes contact, in other words the closer to its horizontal circumference, the more side spin you can put on it. This means that you can use the longer, less lofted clubs when playing with slice spin, which has the added advantage of giving you more length in the shot. This is particularly useful when you have an obstacle fairly close in front but want to play the ball as far past it as possible.

Where you need to control the length of such a shot, you can still use the less lofted clubs in order to gain side spin. But here you will need to hold the club lower down the handle and not swing back so far. With the more lofted clubs, which you would in normal circumstances use for these distances, you will put back spin on the ball and the effect of this will be to eliminate any side spin. Thus the ball will carry straight on in the direction of the swing path, making no side turn at all.

*Where the average golfer would have to be content with just chipping clear of trouble, one with sufficient skill who can turn the ball in the air may save a stroke by sending the ball all the way to the green (RIGHT).*

*Happily not all shots have to be trick ones—and the best shot of all is the one truly struck with the only spin involved being back spin (LEFT), to stop the ball dead on the green.*

## Using gentle spin

There will be occasions where you will not necessarily need to apply a full-bodied spin but simply want to vary the flight of the ball slightly to avoid a possible problem like, for example, overhanging branches on the side of the fairway. In this situation you should still apply some spin – either hook or slice – to the ball, but you do not need to alter the swing for the shot.

The adjustments needed for the shot are very simple. For a slight hook spin you have to move your stance fractionally to the right, closing it slightly to the target line, and closing the face of the club a little. For a slight slice spin, all that is required is to open the club-face a fraction, while turning your stance just off to the left of the target line. The important point to bear in mind with both gentle hooks and slices is that your swing path for both types of shot is only off-line through the mildest of adjustments in your stance. There is a temptation to exaggerate which you must resist.

Having understood the method used to apply a gentle amount of spin, you obviously need to know when to use it. You may be concerned that a particular hazard, although not directly in line with the target, is naggingly close to it and you want to make sure that you do not land in it if your shot is slightly off target. In such a situation, by putting just a little spin on the ball – hook if the obstacle is on the left and slice if it is on the right – you will avoid trouble and end up with the ball on target.

You can also use gentle side spin to counteract the effect of cross winds, since this enables the ball to hold a reasonably straight course as the spin works against the opposing wind. In such a situation, where the wind is blowing from left to right, you need to apply slight hook spin, while if it is blowing from right to left you should neutralize this by playing with a bit of slice spin. Depending on the strength of the wind, the ball is likely to be blown off line altogether unless you take precautions, and this is particularly the case with a lofted club where the height gained makes the ball become vulnerable.

There is always a tendency when opening or closing the face of the club-head to alter the swing plane in the same direction. This happens if you use your forearms to turn the club-head rather than adjusting the club with your hands. You should turn the club-face in or out, as the case may be, resting it on the turf, and *then* take up your grip while insuring the blade remains crooked.

*When only a very mild form of spin is required for the shot, there is no need to alter the swing path. By turning the club in the grip slightly outward (BELOW) or inward (BELOW RIGHT), as the case may be, the ball will turn gently in the air in that direction.*

*Although you may feel that turning the club at address is insufficient, this sequence shows the effect at the top of the back swing. When the club-face lies almost horizontal and is "closed" (ABOVE LEFT), on its return to the ball it will impart spin that will turn the ball to the left. When the toe of the club points directly to the ground (LEFT), once the head returns to the ball it will be "open" from the target line and the ball will turn to the right. To emphasize the point, compare these with the perfect "square" position (ABOVE).*

## Playing on slopes

Slopes and hillsides pose their own particular problems on a golf course since, depending on the lie of the ball, you will be playing the shot with the ball either above or below you. The gradient of the slope will determine the type of shot you can play safely and it is very important that you adopt a realistic attitude as to what can and cannot be done.

You may, for example, be able to play for length where the slope is a gentle one and no major alteration is required to the stance or the position of the ball. But on a steeper slope, where considerable adjustments have to be made, it is suicidal to attempt a bold shot. In such a case you should concentrate more on hitting the ball cleanly and in the right direction. Length in this situation is very much of secondary importance.

## Playing uphill

On a gentle slope you should not have too much of a problem since little adjustment is required in the set-up for the shot. What you have to watch out for in any uphill situation, however, is that you do not hit the ball into the slope.

In normal circumstances it is a natural reaction to lean up the slope in order to maintain your balance. In fact, you need to do just the opposite to insure that when you swing through the ball, the bottom of the swing *feels* parallel to the ground. To achieve this you must have your body at an angle of 90 degrees to the slope and therefore you must lean back slightly. How far you need to lean will depend on the gradient of the slope.

*When playing on a gentle up slope (FAR LEFT), you can afford to be somewhat adventurous and play the shot using a wood.*

*When the slope is more severe, you should pay some regard to your sense of balance. In such a situation you should attempt a more modest shot, using a more lofted club (LEFT).*

Even though you set up with the correct body angle, when you swing, you will instinctively feel the need to lean up the slope. If you do, the chances are you will hit the ball into the ground rather than up into the air. To avoid this you should keep the ball more backward in the stance than usual so that it lies in a more central position.

Equally you should reduce the amount of loft in the club since the ball, if correctly struck, will fly upwards anyway. If you use the same club as you would on flat ground, the ball will fly even higher into the air and you will sacrifice distance unnecessarily. Thus, according to the degree of the slope, always play with one of the longer clubs.

Because of the position of the slope, with the ground rising above you, you will not be able to move your weight forward during the through swing. If you try to, you will almost certainly hit the ball into the slope. However, this causes another problem since without that movement of weight you will tend to pull the ball slightly to the left. To cure this aim fractionally to the right, with your stance turned to the right.

The steeper the slope gets, however, the more lofted the club you should use and the further forward the ball needs to

*Where possible you should attempt to lean with the slope so that your spine is perpendicular to the lie of the ball rather than to the horizon.*

*This will enable you to swing the club up the hill and well into the follow-through, as shown in this sequence (RIGHT, FAR RIGHT).*

be positioned in the stance. Balance, obviously, becomes an increasing problem. To prevent yourself from falling back as you play the shot, you have to start leaning up the slope a little, bending your left knee slightly to do so. This means that you are increasing your chances of crushing the ball into the slope, which is why you need to use a loftier club.

Do not attempt to get too much power into the shot or you will end up losing your balance and pulling the ball well off to the left. Once again, direction is more important than distance.

Where the uphill slope is very steep, the best you can really hope for is to get the ball into play. There should be little or no thought of distance. You will need a short shafted, lofted club and will have to bend your left knee even more to keep your balance. One other way of helping to play this awkward type of shot is to move your hands down the handle of the club to reduce the length of the swing, which of necessity will be more of an upward pull of the club rather than a flowing movement.

## Playing downhill

Where the slope is a gentle one, you should experience few difficulties in playing the ball. Again you must insure that your body is as near as possible at 90 degrees to the ground, while still maintaining a good balance. By leaning down the slope you should avoid the obvious problem of catching the ground behind the ball with the club as you swing it down and through.

Since your weight will be shifting down the slope – and therefore into the shot – you can afford to have the ball slightly further forward in the stance. Do not overdo this, however, since if you get the bottom of the swing too far behind the ball you are likely to hit the ground before the ball.

By swinging down the slope you will find that, with the club you would normally choose, the ball tends to fly too low. To gain extra height, use the club with the next loft up. This will also help to prevent you from putting slice spin on the ball.

The steeper the down slope, the more you need to lean up the hill, with the majority of your weight on your right foot, and to bend your right knee. You will

*When playing down a gentle slope, you are well advised to use a club with more loft (RIGHT); wooden clubs should be avoided under such circumstances.*

*As the slope gets steeper, you must make sure that the ball is positioned much further back in the stance (LEFT).*

also need to move the ball back in the stance to reduce the chances of hitting the ground behind it with the club on the down swing.

To avoid contact with the ground, make the swing steeper so that your club-head comes down on the ball from a much sharper angle. By doing this, you can afford to use quite a lofted club in order to send the ball confidently away from the slope.

In extreme cases, as with the uphill slope, there is no point in trying to be ambitious with the shot. You must therefore forget all about distance and concentrate on getting the ball away in the right direction. The danger of hitting the ground behind the ball is even greater now and it will be not so much a case of swinging down into the shot but chopping at the ball. Therefore you need a very lofted club, probably the sand iron.

You must bend your right knee even more and also keep the ball well back in the stance. Control of the run of the ball when it lands will be minimal, since it is impossible to apply any back spin. However, it is far better to overrun the shot than to trickle it down the slope and watch it come to a standstill further down.

*When playing down a severe slope (RIGHT), lean with the slope so that your spine is as near perpendicular to the lie of the ball as possible. This will allow you a steep back swing and a long through swing.*

## Playing along a slope

The same criteria apply in this situation as when playing the ball up or down a slope. Balance is crucial and you should concentrate on hitting the ball accurately and in the right direction, rather than trying to gain too much distance.

Where the ball is above you on the slope, you must settle your body weight back slightly so that you feel at an angle of 90 degrees to the ground. This means the swing will be flatter and because of the fractional upward tilt of the toe of the club-head the ball will tend to fly off to the left. To compensate for this you must aim the shot off to the right of the target. The exact amount of this compensatory aim will largely depend on how steep the slope is.

Regardless of the type of club you are using, take up your stance with the ball positioned in the center. You must keep your back as near upright as possible and, with steeper slopes, you may have to move your hands further down the club-handle in order to keep your balance. In extreme cases, you will have to use a more lofted club than normal,

*The most difficult slope to play from is one where the ball lies below the level of your feet (RIGHT). Leaning forward, as you must, results in the turn of the body being restricted. This in turn creates a steepness in the swing plane. In these circumstances it is better to settle for a more lofted club and be less ambitious over the final length of the shot.*

which has a shorter handle. If this is the case, you must be prepared to sacrifice length for accuracy.

When the ball is lying below you on the slope, you must bring your body forward but at the same time maintain your balance. This is not easy, particularly when swinging into the shot, since there is always some forward momentum and this, added to the direction of the slope, will tend to give you a toppling feeling. On severe slopes you can assist in gaining a reasonable position by bending your knees, although you will soon know when you have reached your limit.

You will find that if you use the normal shoulder turn in this situation you will start to fall forward. To avoid this the swing needs to be controlled much more with the arms and hands. With limited body turn the club will tend to swing more across the ball and you will therefore need to position the ball forward slightly. Usually the ball has a habit of slicing off to the right of the target so you must adjust your aim accordingly. The spin you will achieve from the more lofted clubs does tend, however, to correct this.

*The easier slope to play from is one where the ball lies above the level of your feet (RIGHT).*

*The correct way to play this type of shot is to reduce the length of the club by going down the handle and, using a very flat swing plane, to hit the ball with greater enthusiasm.*

## Playing out of bunkers

It is every golfer's intention when out on the course to avoid, wherever possible, the many problem areas that are strategically placed to add complexity to the holes. Inevitably, however, you will find yourself trapped in one every so often and the problem then is how to escape. Bunkers are certainly not the friendliest of hazards and special techniques are required to get the ball safely out of the sand.

How you go about this will depend to a large extent on the lie of the ball in the sand. Sometimes you may be fortunate enough to find that it has ended up on top of the sand. In this situation you should be able to play a splash shot to get it back onto the fairway or up to the green. Depending on how soft the sand is and how hard the ball has dropped into it, you may be faced with the situation where the ball has partly buried itself. In this case, the problem of removing it is that much more difficult. Harder still, however, is when this situation is combined with the fact that the ball has landed on a slope in the bunker.

There is, however, a special iron to help you cope with the specific problems of hitting out of the sand. The design of the sand iron, which has the greatest angle of loft of all the clubs in the set and also a wider base than normal, offers you a great deal of assistance. But much also depends on how well you can adjust your normal techniques and how accurately you can strike the ball.

*The ability to swing confidently through the ball, while maintaining an open club-face, is the key to a successful bunker shot (RIGHT).*

*You can cover comparatively long distances from fairway bunkers, provided that the ball is well away from the face of the bunker (ABOVE). Nevertheless, there is always the fear of making contact with the sand before the ball, so overly ambitious long carries should never be attempted.*

**On the level** Where the ball is sitting on top of the sand, several changes are needed from the methods you would use to play a normal shot with a lofted club. Instead of attempting to make contact directly with the face of the ball, you actually have to aim the point of strike a fraction behind the ball. The result is that you have a small cushion of sand between the club-head and the ball at the point of impact.

Because you want to get maximum lift on the ball, you have to hit across it rather than straight through it. This is done by positioning the ball forward in the stance and aiming the line of the feet and the shoulders off to the left. To play the shot you must swing back and then through as fully as you can, being aware that the swinging arc is upright. This is to insure that the ball lifts. The speed at which you bring the club down will determine how far forward the ball will go.

When playing out of a fairway – as opposed to greenside – bunker, you will obviously be hoping for reasonable length and should therefore bring the club through fairly quickly. However, you must make sure that the pace remains constant through the swing, since if you speed up the swing partway though you are almost certain to misdirect the ball.

When playing out of a deep bunker alongside the green, you will want much more height and very little length in the shot. Therefore you must swing the club more slowly. Another way of softening the flight is to have the ball extremely well forward in the stance – which should be turned left even more – and

*Unlike the procedure for deep greenside bunkers, it is best not to bury your feet in the sand, since this encourages contact with the sand before the ball. It is advisable to hold the club down the handle a little, which firms up the wrist action and ensures a clean contact (LEFT).*

*This sequence (RIGHT) illustrates a perfect splash shot out of the bunker. The club-head, which is kept open throughout, travels across the target line from out to in, catching the sand just before the ball.*

to open the face of the club-head. You need not worry too much about the ball running on after it lands on the green. In fact, the small cushion of sand is just as capable of putting back spin on the ball as the club-head is.

It is important to remember that you must never be too ambitious with a shot out of a bunker. If you pay too much attention to sending the ball as far as possible, you may well end up mis-hitting it and quite probably leaving it in the bunker. The golden rule, however the ball is placed in the bunker, is to get it out. Concern about the length of the shot must always come second.

If the ball is partly buried in the sand, you will have to force it out. In order to strike well down to the bottom of the ball, the club-head needs to be swung into the sand before it makes contact. How far before will depend on how deep the ball is lying. What you should be aiming for is to strike the ball as the club-head reaches the lowest point of the swing, and this is something you will have to judge for yourself.

Because you are swinging into the sand, you need to lower yourself slightly into it as well. To achieve this, you just have to shuffle your feet about until they sink in. In this way you should guarantee striking the ball low down. If you do not sink your feet into the sand, you are likely to hit over the top of the ball.

When you take up your stance for this shot, stand square on to the target line and have the ball positioned in the center of the stance. You will need a strong, full swing into the ball to get it

out. You cannot hope for much control over the ball, which is unlikely to lift very high and will tend to run on some way after landing. This is because there will be little or no back spin on the ball.

The simplest way to hit the ball when it is lying on wet sand is to adopt the techniques for playing a pitch shot (see page 180). In fact, you may find it easier to use a pitching wedge rather than a sand iron in these circumstances. You should aim to hit the sand just before the ball. The ball will fly lower, unless you can keep the club-face open, and you will have little control over the forward momentum once it lands.

*To play a splash shot, address the ball with the blade lying slightly open (LEFT, BELOW). Since the stance is open, the club will travel across the ball, helping to weaken its forward flight, yet increasing its lift.*

*When the ball is plugged in the sand (BOTTOM LEFT), you need to take up a square stance. Line the club-head up square with the ball in a central position, and hit through the sand (BOTTOM).*

*Although it may appear to be quite simple, a bunker shot from an uphill slope (RIGHT) is one that even professionals dislike.*

**On a slope** When you have to play up the slope of a bunker, you have the same problems as on a grass slope but with the added complication that there is sand to contend with.

You cannot play the basic splash shot here since there would be no cushion of sand between the club-head and the ball. The best way to overcome this problem is to lean with the slope so that, in effect, you are playing the shot on flat ground. This allows you to create that cushion of sand you need.

Similar problems exist when you have to play down the slope of a bunker, although here the trouble is that you often bury the club-head in the sand too early. The result is that when it reaches the ball it strikes too high up. The solution is to lean as much with the slope as possible, use a very steep swing and come down firmly just behind the ball, which you should have well back in the stance. The best you can really hope for is for the ball to fly out of the bunker. You will not get any height on the ball and without back spin you will not be able to control its forward momentum once it has landed.

*The danger with this type of shot is that the blade of the club will make contact with the ball too cleanly. The correct procedure is to lean your body with the slope (ABOVE LEFT) so that it is possible to take some sand before you strike the ball, but at the same time avoid burying the club-head in the slope (LEFT).*

*By far the most difficult bunker shot is that where the ball lies on a down slope (RIGHT). Although it is very difficult to lean with the slope, every effort should be made to do so.*

*Pick the club up very sharply on the back swing (LEFT) so that you can make an unnaturally steep delivery across the ball (BELOW).*

## The short game

So far we have assumed that, either from the tee or the fairway, you have approached the green with a long-range shot and succeeded. However, there are bound to be occasions when your approach shot lands up just short or wide of the green, whether by accident or design, and you are not close enough or the ground is not good enough for you to use your putter. (This club should always be the first choice, wherever possible.)

When faced with this situation, your objective should be to get the ball as close to the hole as you can, thus hopefully saving you that extra putt and another stroke at the hole. To do this, you need to play either a pitch shot or a chip shot.

The basic difference between these shots is that when pitching you lift the ball well up in the air and aim to make it stop quickly on landing. When chipping, there is less height on the ball and more run. In principle you should play the former the further away you are from the hole and the latter the closer you are to the hole.

## Pitch shots

Because of the distance you need to carry the ball in the air, this shot requires a lot more momentum than you would use when chipping the ball. To play it you should have a special club in your set designed for just this job – the pitching wedge, which has the necessary high degree of loft on the club-face.

There are some important differences in the stance you must adopt for

*Success in golf depends not just on massive drives but on accurate and consistent pitch shots (RIGHT).*

the pitch shot. Your feet should be very close together with the ball positioned in the center of the stance, which should be square to the line of the shot. When you take up the grip, your hands must be fairly well down the handle. Instead of passing the club across to the left hand, you in fact use the reverse procedure and bring the left hand back, keeping the shaft of the club almost vertical. This is one of the very few exceptions to the basic rule of taking up the grip, which you should already have learned (see page 54).

In this position, you may very well feel that most of the work needed to play the shot can be done with the hands and wrists. Unfortunately, if you let them do so you will almost certainly misdirect the shot, particularly over longer distances. You must, as with a normal long shot, concentrate on swinging back and then through the ball with an adequate involvement of body movement.

The length of your swing is all important, since this will establish how far the ball travels in the air. Only by practicing with a number of balls, bringing the club further back each time and increasing the body movement, will you discover exactly what length of swing you need. This will depend on the distance you want to send the ball and what increase in power is required for the shot.

Back spin is important with this type of shot and you can add to its effect by

*At the point where the distance to be covered by a shot is less than the maximum carry of your shortest club, then the part-swing comes into play. The ability to control and balance movements so that each part of the swing blends in with the others is crucial to the success of this type of short play—as is clearly demonstrated in this sequence (RIGHT).*

speeding up your swing just before contact with the ball. The steeper the angle of flight, the quicker the ball will stop on landing. To achieve this you must make the angle of your swing steeper and you can do so by standing with your feet closer together and by bringing your grip nearer to the top of the club. This induces additional wrist action and will insure that the face of the club-head opens and hits across the lower part of the ball at the point of strike.

Pitching the ball accurately is a vital part of every golfer's repertoire, not least because it can ease the problems you may otherwise face with putting by cutting down on the number of shots required on the green.

*One of the best ways of moderating the length and enthusiasm of the swing is to narrow the width of the stance and soften the legs. This will automatically reduce the width of the swing (LEFT, ABOVE).*

*When you are faced with the problem of playing the ball from a very poor lie, more thought must be given to the hand and wrist action. Although it takes a great deal of practice to gain suitable finesse in the shot, you will find it is well worth the effort (LEFT, ABOVE).*

*Where the ball lies awkwardly and a straightforward shot is out of the question, the advantage of a sophisticated hand action becomes apparent (RIGHT, BELOW).*

*When faced with a delicate pitch shot with the ball buried in deep grass, narrow your stance and introduce a greater flexibility. This will enable you to reduce the swing arc and accelerate the club steeply into the ball to lift it out (LEFT).*

## Chip shot

The chip shot comes into its own when you are close to the green and it is unnecessary to pitch the ball up to the hole. The principle behind it is to loft the ball over the final yards of rough ground and land it on the green, allowing it to run or toward the hole. Depending on the conditions and where you happen to be playing from, you will need to adjust to the appropriate club for the distance the ball flies in the air and how far it has to run along the ground. This involves careful club selection, whereby you use the less lofted irons when you want less flight and more run, and the more lofted ones when additional flight and less run is required. Although it is possible to establish very general rules about the effect of chipping with clubs of varying lofts, the only accurate way of assessing this is to practice the shot yourself, working through the range of lofted irons.

Bearing in mind that you will be running the ball across the green, you need to check on the green just as you would when putting. This will affect where you aim for – either at the hole or to one side of it, depending on whether the green is flat or sloping. When you take up the stance, your feet should be only a few inches apart and the ball should be backward of center. Your whole body must be square on to the line of the shot.

Keep your left hand well forward and bring the club across to it when taking up the grip. Your hands should be well down the handle of the club. In this position the club will, in fact, be leaning toward the target and the weight of your body will be very much on the left side.

With the chip shot, as with the putt, body movement should be almost nonexistent. Obviously you will have to move your shoulders slightly to create the necessary swing in the club and provide the right momentum, but there should be little or no body movement elsewhere.

The key point about this type of shot is that the trajectory of the ball must be kept fairly low. If there is any extra movement in the arms and a fuller swing, you will inevitably lift the ball too high in the air. The height that the loft of the club will offer should be quite sufficient to enable you to clear the rough ground safely. The straighter the face of the club you use, the less momentum you require. With too much pace on the ball, it will fly too far forward and race on across the green, probably overshooting the hole.

There are occasions when you need to play a lofted shot and stop the ball running, but do not have the necessary distance to play a normal pitch shot. What you want is a combination of the two. Regard the shot as a chip shot, but make sure the ball is much further forward in the stance than usual and bring your grip up nearer to the top of the handle. Using a very lofted iron, play as for a chip shot but reduce the momentum in the swing a fraction.

You may find yourself in a position

*The less you try to do when chipping, the better the results. Here the club is moved forward and through the ball, allowing the loft of the club-face to determine the lift of the ball (LEFT, ABOVE).*

where you cannot bounce the ball onto the green, but have to do so well short of it. Alternatively, you may be in a position where you cannot or do not want to lift the ball too high but have to achieve good distance, for example when playing into the wind and across a good fairway. What you need here is in effect an extended chip shot. Drop down a club or two from the pitching wedge and widen your stance keeping the ball backward of center. Although your weight should be on the left side, with your left hand forward and the club leaning toward the target, use a short aggresive movement instead of playing the normal gentle chip shot. Your hands, incidentally, should be reasonably well down the grip of the club. You will also have to involve some body movement and increase the amount you turn your shoulders. How much you do this will depend on how far you want to send the ball.

The benefit of being able to adapt the short shot – whether it is basically a pitch or a chip – is that it opens up many possibilities in terms of where you can play the ball. Proper ball control around the green will pay great dividends, particularly in adverse weather where you have had to sacrifice strokes on the fairway. A good pitch or chip shot at the right time can pull back holes that might otherwise have been lost, or gain you valuable extra strokes over the course of a round. It is a part of the game of golf well worth practising and refining.

*Even though the lie is slightly downhill, the simplicity in the swing movement makes the shot look rather like a long putt. Only the slight lateral movement of the body, which insures that the club hits the ball cleanly, differentiates this chip shot from a putting stroke (ABOVE RICHT).*

## Playing in poor weather

As if the techniques of golf and the design of the course do not provide a great enough challenge to the player, very often the weather does its best to test one's ability even further. Wind and rain are the two most obvious enemies and either can create havoc with your game if you are not able to make the necessary adjustments and treat each with respect.

Learning to cope with the adverse conditions such elements can provide is important, since there is nothing worse than for morale to be sapped and your game to collapse. Inevitably you will drop strokes. You would not be human if you did not. But as long as you can keep these to a minimum and learn to accept this, you should be able to keep your spirits up and your game going.

## Playing in the rain

Obviously there are limits as to how bad the conditions must be before it becomes impossible to play on. There is no way that you can play a ball through great pools of water, for example. If you do find yourself in one, then you are allowed to take relief, according to the rules. Equally, on the greens you are not expected to putt through a lake. In this situation you can move your ball to a spot that offers a dry passage through to the hole, provided this is a similar distance from the hole as before.

It hardly needs stating that you will get a much poorer contact between a wet club-head and a wet ball than you

*Playing in the rain can be a thoroughly demoralizing experience, but even top professionals like Severiano Ballesteros (RIGHT) have to grin and bear it. If you have a caddy it is a good idea to take advantage of whatever shelter you can get when lining up a shot.*

Slazenger
SUN
ALLIANCE
PGA
CHAMPIONSHIP
46
Ballesteros
Slazenger

*If you find your route to the hole blocked by a large pool of water (ABOVE), you are allowed to take relief by moving your ball to a drier spot the same distance away from the hole.*

will with a dry one. While you can keep the club-head dry by wiping it with a towel before you use it, you are not allowed to keep wiping the ball. The only time this is permitted is when you are starting each hole. After drying it before a tee shot, you cannot do so again until you are on the green.

The moral behind this, therefore, is to keep the ball in the air as much as possible. This means using a more lofted club than you would normally use in dry conditions. Because of this, you will have to sacrifice length and therefore maybe a stroke at the longer holes. This is going to prove a lot less expensive, however, over the course of a round than attempting longer shots that run and run, allowing the ball to get wetter and muddier. Another significant point to bear in mind is that with the straighter-faced clubs the ball is more likely to skid off when the club-head is wet.

One small bonus when it is wet, however, is that the greens become softer and therefore tend to hold the ball back more. This allows you to play much stronger shots to the green and be more positive with your putting, safe in the knowledge that the ball is unlikely to run on far, if at all.

Having considered the problems posed for the clubs and the ball, what about the player? If the lower standard of golf is not enough to try your patience and dampen your spirits, then the feeling of being soaked through to the skin certainly will. Be prepared when you go out on the course, particularly if rain is forecast. In the two or three hours you are likely to be playing the round, the weather can change dramatically and it does not take long for rain to soak your clothes.

Take a waterproof suit with you and a change of glove, since you will make stroke play even harder if your grip keeps slipping on the greasy handle. Wear good spiked shoes to give you the best possible grip with your feet and a cap to protect your head. Keep several towels and dry cloths in your golf bag, as well, so that you can wipe the clubs each time you use them. Headcovers will help protect your clubs from the rain while they are kept in the bag.

## Playing in the wind

However hard and accurately you strike the ball, the presence of a strong wind is bound to affect its flight. Wind is a constant problem on the golf course, particularly on the coastal links where you can always expect some breeze off the sea.

A further problem on such courses is that there is normally little shelter in the way of trees or rising ground. Even on inland courses, where there is this type of shelter, once the ball is in the air the wind will catch it and blow it about. In addition, there is still the chance that the wind will be blowing up or down the fairway, creating a tunnel effect.

Playing in windy conditions is a skill

that even a moderate golfer can master. With this skill much advantage can be gained over generally better players who find themselves struggling to control the ball. It is basically a question of recognizing the strengths and weaknesses in your own game and playing to them.

In most cases there will be a choice – to take advantage of the prevailing conditions and play with the wind or to go on the attack and try playing against it in the hope of neutralizing its effect on the particular shot. There is no easy answer as to which method will work best. Only experience and an understanding of your own capabilities will teach you when to play defensively and when to play aggressively.

**Following wind** You get an obvious feeling of cooperation when the wind is blowing from directly behind you, since it will help you carry the ball further than you would normally be able to hit it. However, this advantage can only be obtained by lofting the shot. The higher you can send the ball, the more help the wind can give, so use a club with more loft than you would normally choose.

Before you rush to enlist the help of the wind, bear in mind how much further the ball is likely to travel and where you hope it will land. The extra length you gain with the help of the wind may now put you in range of hazards that you would normally not have reached. There is little point in going for those extra yards if this means winding up in a stream or bunker – or even running off a fairway where it bends to the left or right in a dogleg. If you are concerned that the extra distance could put you in trouble then use a shorter club.

A following wind can pose special problems at short holes. Bearing in mind the siting of bunkers to trap the unwary, with the wind increasing the distance of your shot, the margin of error when aiming onto the green is greatly reduced. A further difficulty you may experience is trying to control the ball when it lands and preventing it from racing right across the green. One way of restricting the run of the ball after it has landed is to play the ball higher and softer. Because it will then come down at a steeper angle and at less pace, it should not run on too far. The loftier the club, the greater help it will be, as will the use of a slightly raised tee peg. In any case, even if the ball does run to the back end of the green, the longer putt will be a lot easier and safer to play than trying to hit a plugged ball out of the sand. The answer is not to be too ambitious and, when in doubt, play safe.

So far only the benefits of a following wind have been discussed and, of course, these should be used to your advantage as much and as often as possible. But this type of wind does have its disadvantages, too. And these are no more clearly demonstrated than when playing a short shot to the green. Here ball control is all important and the effect of the following wind works completely against this.

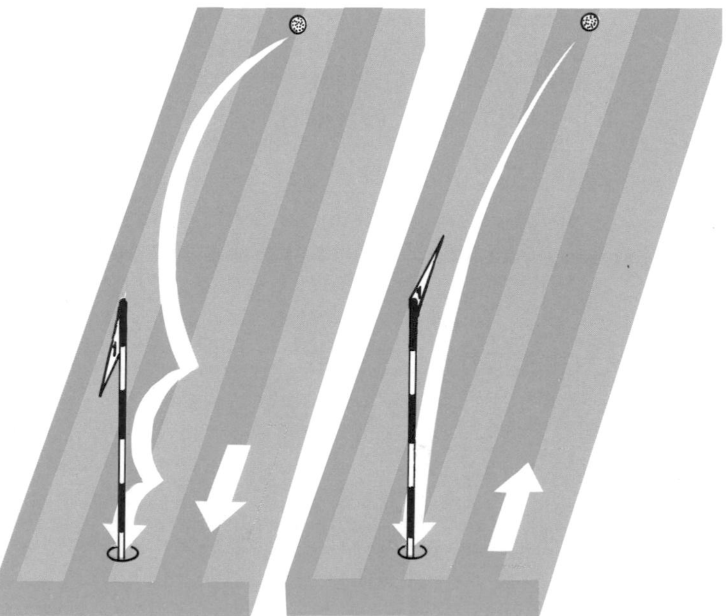

*The consolation of playing a shot into the wind is the knowledge that all short iron shots will stop immediately on landing. This means that the ball can be hit firmly right up to the flag (ABOVE).*

*When playing with a following wind, you should aim to land the ball short of the target so that it may run on up to the flag (ABOVE LEFT).*

The real trouble with the following wind, as already mentioned, is that it has a habit of neutralizing any back spin you put on the ball, which is the essential ingredient of a short shot because it enables the ball to stop virtually dead on the green. The way to get around this dilemma is to use a very lofted club, such as a pitching wedge, or even, where there is sufficient grass underneath, a sand iron. By using one of these clubs you can get maximum height with minimum pace on the ball and increase the chances of the ball stopping soon after landing.

Remember too, the other methods already discussed for increasing the loft of a shot. These include having the ball fairly forward in the stance so that your shoulders are lined up slightly more open and your club swings down and through from outside to inside the line of the shot.

**Head wind** This type of wind makes life very difficult for the golfer. The natural reaction is to force the ball that much harder to counteract the effect of the wind blowing against the flight. Of course this approach is fraught with dangers, since by trying to hit harder you are likely to introduce or exaggerate faults in the swing.

Some people think that by keeping the ball on a lower trajectory this will help minimize the effect of the wind. As a result, they turn the club-face in at the address to reduce its loft. But by reducing the loft, you risk ballooning the shot.

There is no simple solution to this problem. What you must resign yourself to is the fact that length will be lost in the wind and you must be prepared to drop the odd stroke at the longer holes. As a general guide, particularly when playing off the tee, aim to get a bit of hook spin on the ball, since this will help it to run on further after landing. This entails having the ball further back when you take up your stance, with your shoulders lining up fractionally closed to the line of the shot.

What you must avoid at all costs is putting any slice spin on the ball, which will happen if the ball is too far forward in the stance. If you do, you will sacrifice even more length in the shot. Equally, avoid putting any back spin on the ball. Since the rotation of the ball is with the wind, the net effect will be to hold the ball up longer and again valuable distance will be lost. To play safe, it may be worth dropping your hands down the club-handle fractionally to shorten the swing. The effect of this is to eliminate wrist activity and give greater control.

A strong head wind can work in your favor at some short holes or when you are playing a short shot to the green. In either case, the wind will hold the ball up and add to the effect of any back spin by preventing the ball from running forward after it has landed on the green.

With your tee shot to the shorter holes, you can safely use a club with a lot less loft than you would normally and aim for the green, confident in the knowledge that the head wind will hold the ball and cause it to descend sharply. The only danger you face is that should the ball fall short of the target and drop into a bunker, it will do so steeply and present you with additional problems if it plugs in the sand.

Where you are faced with a short shot to the green, you can afford to play a firm stroke and use a short swing. It is best to move your grip down the handle and keep the ball positioned reasonably well back in the stance. In this way you should be able to guarantee good control, plenty of loft and back spin which, helped by the direction of the wind, will stop the ball on landing.

It could be, on a long hole, that you need to gain maximum distance from your second shot. In this situation you can use one of the fairway woods and swing with your grip moved slightly down the handle.

**Cross wind** The problem with cross winds is not so much one of length, but rather direction. If you play a normal straight shot with little or no spin, the wind is bound to move the ball off line to the left or right, depending on where it is blowing from.

With the wind coming from the left, you can expect the ball to be blown to the right of the intended line of the shot. Moreover, what is worse is that a strong cross wind, which is blowing against your back, tends to push your body forward and too much over the ball. From this position you are quite likely to slice the shot, thus exaggerating the problem. One way to counteract this is to use a loftier club and put some hook spin on

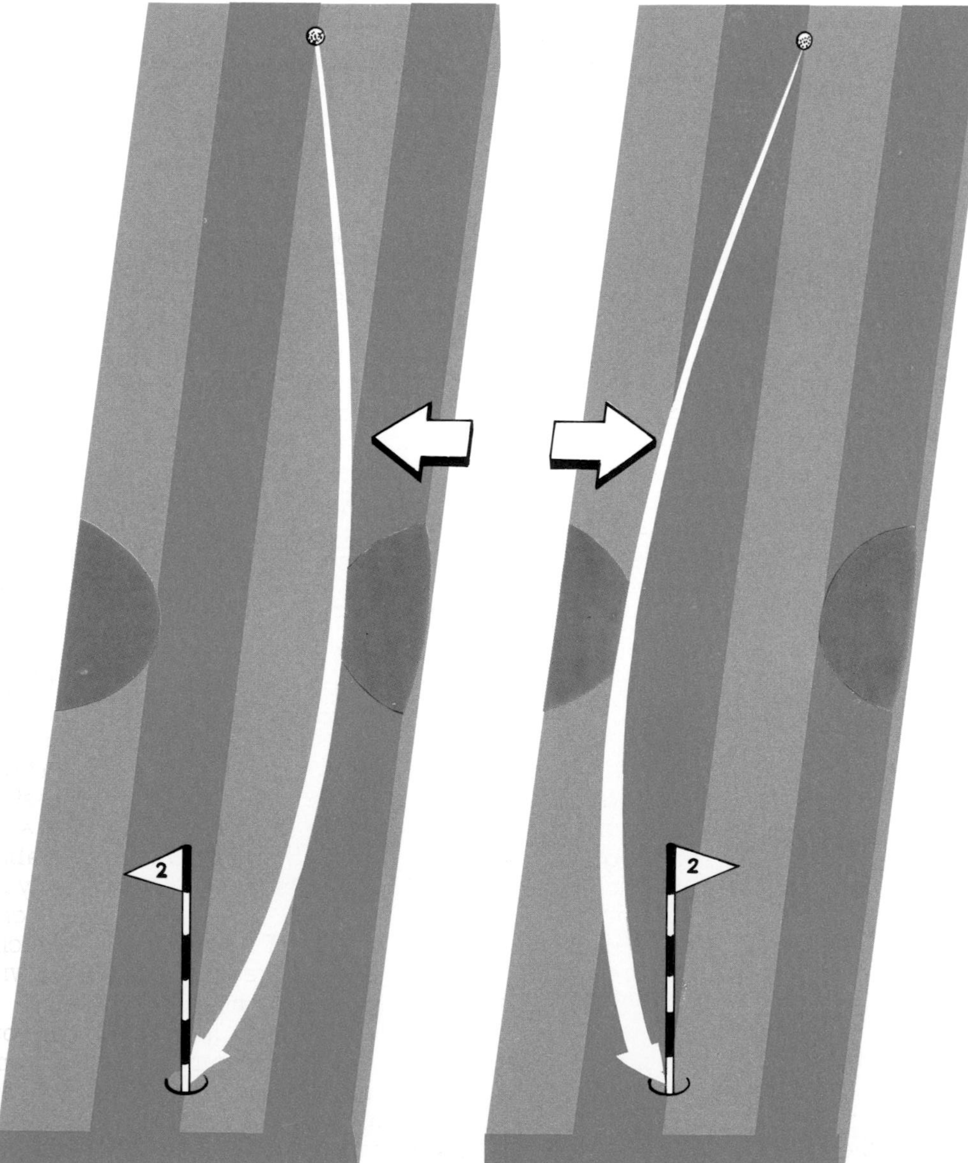


*Cross winds cannot be ignored on the golf course. You must either aim toward the wind and allow the ball to be blown back with it, or you must apply the appropriate spin on the ball to fight it.*

the ball. This helps to keep the ball pulling to the left against the wind and thus, hopefully, maintain a direct course to the target. This is fine when you are playing with an iron – and it is to a degree possible with the more lofted woods, but you should not attempt to hook the ball with a driver, since this club has too little loft.

The alternative to hook spin – and one you may decide it is easier to adopt in all situations of this kind – is to aim the ball fractionally off to the left and leave the wind to bring it back on line with the target. How far off line you decide to aim will depend on how strong the wind is at the time and how much deviation it is likely to cause to the ball.

When the wind blows the other way – from the right and into the player – there are generally fewer problems to contend with. This is particularly true with the longer shots, where by aiming off to the right of the target you can afford to play a full-blooded shot and leave the wind to push it back on line.

Life on the golf course, however, is not so easy when you are playing onto the green, since it is hard to control the ball in a right to left wind and prevent it from running on too far. In this situation there are two fairly simple choices. You can play short of the green to cut down the margin of error and leave yourself a chip shot to the hole.

Alternatively, you can aim for the front of the green, accepting the fact that the ball will almost certainly run on and end up at the back, possibly leaving you with a longish putt back to the hole. In either case, you will need to adjust your aim and play to the right of your target – that is, into the wind.

If you feel sufficiently confident to play the shot with some hook spin and so gain extra distance, then use a club with slightly more loft and take up your stance with the ball positioned further

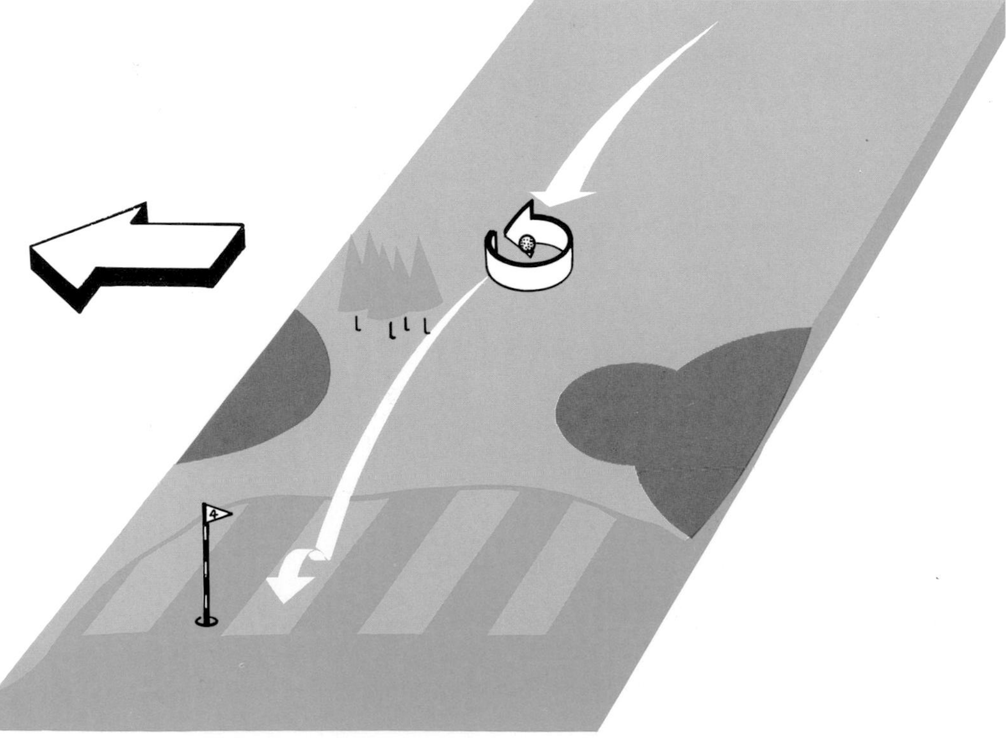

*A cross wind blowing from the left not only poses a threat to the ball's flight but also tends to push you forward over the ball. By using hook spin (RIGHT) you can counteract this threat and take a relatively straight course down the fairway.*

back than normal. By playing the shot out into the wind, and adding your hook technique, the ball should then fly back in a big curve onto its course with the help of the spin.

Those players who can control slice spin have the option of using it here and can, in that situation, aim directly at the target with a less lofted club.

**Windy greens** Putting in windy conditions can pose problems. Depending on the length of the shot, some adjustment to the line you take should be made. Where there is a slope and the wind is blowing down it, you need to increase the amount of borrow. Conversely, with the wind against the slope, you can afford to reduce it.

A head wind on the green should cause no trouble and, in fact, can be of definite help since it allows you to play a much firmer, more positive shot to the hole. The worst situation is where you are putting down a slope and the wind is blowing from behind you. Then you have to judge the pace of the ball very carefully or you will find it racing away past the hole to the other side of the green.

Extra care should be taken when playing short shots onto the green. Although you may not be sending the ball very far, thus giving the wind less time to affect its line, the height of the shot can make the ball vulnerable. Thus you should avoid, as far as possible, floating the ball too much in the air.

Depending on the direction of the wind, the ball may pull up more quickly when the wind is against you. Equally it will run on more with the wind behind. It may in some situations be better to play a shorter chip shot and let the ball run toward the hole, rather than attempt to pitch it right up to the hole and misjudge the reaction of the wind.

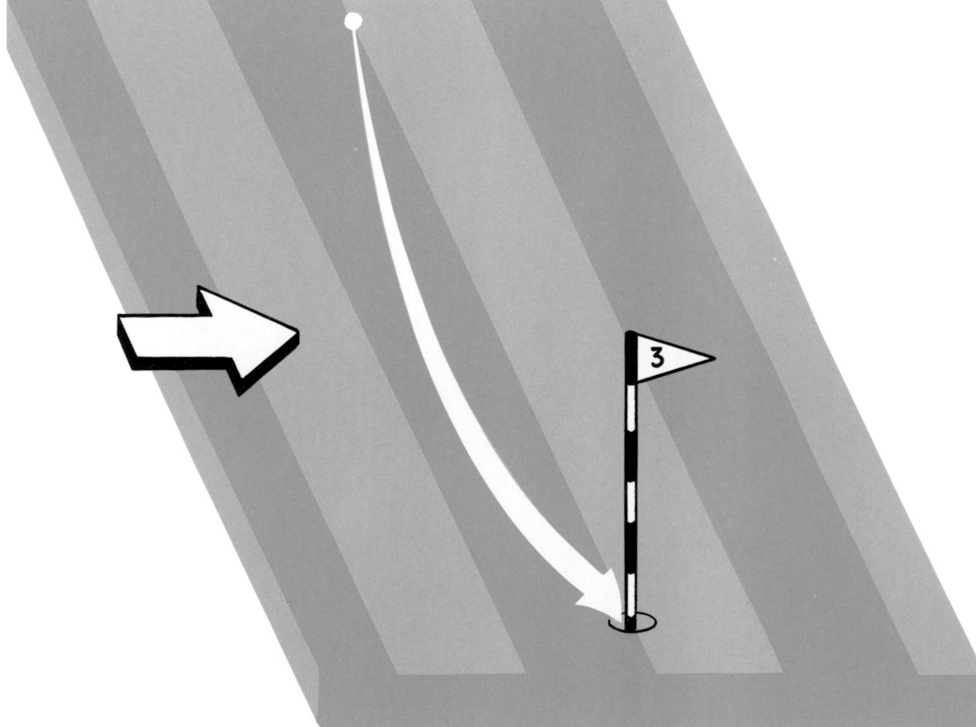


*There is a tendency to believe that once the ball is on the green the wind will no longer have any effect. This is not the case. One of the most difficult shots to judge is that where the wind is blowing in the same direction as the borrow on the green. The combination of the ball taking the slope and being encouraged from behind by a gale can add drastically to its roll (LEFT).*

## Playing out of trouble

A golf course can seem like an impenetrable maze when you are playing badly. Yet when all is going well, you may almost forget that any obstacles exist. The fact is that every stroke can prove troublesome, since that is the way the holes have been designed.

Right from your first shot off the tee, life can prove difficult if you mishit or misdirect the ball. It could land you in awkward rough ground on either side of the fairway or end up behind a tree or other shrub. Ditches, streams and even lakes often provide further hazards and there is always a chance of getting an unlucky lie, where the ball is caught in a branch or sits in a divot or rut. Just in case you avoid all these hazards, there are always bunkers ready to trap your ball, if not on the fairway then certainly at the edge of the green.

The methods for tackling some of these problems have already been covered. These include the techniques required to play the ball out of the sand and also to use spin to bend the flight of the ball around a potential hazard. The following are some of the methods you can adopt to approach the other major troublespots on the course, which include the various types of rough ground, obstacles such as trees and shrubs, water hazards and poor lies.

**Rough** As with any other problem area, it is vital that you do actually get the ball out of rough ground. You must concentrate on this, even at the expense of distance and, in some cases, the ideal direction.

Naturally you must first assess how much of a problem the rough is proving. If the lie is not too deep and the ground cover not too thick, a slightly more lofted club than normal may well suffice. In this situation you can still play the shot with a reasonable amount of power in the swing. The more testing the lie, the more loft you need and the less swing. What

you do not want to see is the ball blasted even further into the rough, so always play for position.

Hit down on the ball to give yourself maximum lift in the shot and to prevent the club-head getting caught in the rough before it makes contact with the ball. Having the ball further back in the stance will help you to achieve this.

Give some thought as to your ideal route out of trouble so that you gain a reasonable line for your next shot. If in any doubt, discretion is definitely the better part of valor, so look for the safest route back to the fairway, even if it does mean playing an extra stroke to reach the green.

*The difficulty of playing from thick grass is that no matter what you do some grass must come into contact with the blade of the club before it gets to the ball. The secret is to use a club with plenty of loft and weight, and then steepen the swing (FAR LEFT). If you use a club with insufficient loft, a substantial cushion of grass comes between it and the ball (LEFT). This may well result in the club embedding itself in the grass (BELOW LEFT) and inhibiting a smooth through swing.*

**Obstacles** Depending on where these lie in relation to the ball, you must decide between the various options open. As long as there is some ground between the ball and the obstacle, you may be able to play over it or certainly around it. But if you want to play over the obstacle, the higher it is the further away the ball will have to be. If the obstacle is very close to the ball, then you may well have to find a route underneath it that will provide you with a suitable escape.

When playing over the top of an obstacle, you must assess the height required on the flight of the ball very carefully. It could be that you will get sufficient loft by playing with the club you would normally use for an unimpeded shot. (It is remarkable how high a standard shot does climb.) Otherwise you will need a more lofted club and must then be prepared to sacrifice some length.

Stand with your feet slightly nearer together than usual and open the stance a bit, keeping the position of the ball well forward. Move your hands up the handle, as well. When you want to increase the loft a little more but still retain reasonable length, instead of choosing a more lofted club increase your swing as required by using a fuller turn of the shoulders and add to the activity in your wrist work.

An alternative could be to play the ball around the obstacle and this means the choice of playing with either hook or slice spin. The main advantage of hook spin is that you have a wider range of clubs at your disposal.

As previously explained (see page 152), one of the easiest ways of putting hook spin on the ball is to aim slightly to the right of the target, turn the club-face fractionally inward and then swing as normal directly down the line of the shot. When playing with slice spin, you need to use a straighter-faced club. Remember that with this shot you must hit across the ball with the club-face slightly open.

*You can go around obstacles, over obstacles or under obstacles—but never believe you can go through obstacles (ABOVE).*

Which type of spin you use will depend on which side of the obstacle you want – or have – to send the ball. To bend it around the right side you need to apply hook spin, while to bend it around the left side you have to use slice spin. Where possible, always play to the right of the obstacle, since hook spin is a lot easier to use than slice spin.

*The advantage of being able to control the spinning ball can make the difference between dropping a shot or playing to par. Here hook spin is applied to bend the ball around the trees, leaving it a clear path to the green (LEFT).*

The other route is under the obstacle. Before you attempt this, however, make sure that you can clear the problem safely. The rise on the ball can be deceptive and hitting the lower branches of a tree, for example, would be disastrous. Probably the safest technique in this kind of situation is to play a chip-and-run shot.

As far as the normal chip shot is concerned, your feet should be slightly wider apart than usual, with the ball well back in the stance. Your left hand needs to stay well forward with the club-face aimed directly at the target. Bring the club down quite steeply, with more of a chopping action. Once the ball has been knocked under and clear of the obstacle, it can then run safely on its way.

*If you are unfortunate enough to find your ball resting in a divot (ABOVE), so that the base of the ball is clearly below the surface, use a club with more loft and play with it positioned back in the stance. You will have to use more of a chopping action so that the club-head drives down and through the ball (ABOVE RIGHT).*

**Water** One hazard, which is not only uncomfortable to play the ball out of but also very awkward, is water. Yet it is certainly worth investigating the possibility of playing the ball rather than incurring a penalty and dropping it clear. This decision will, of course, depend on what advantage there might be in playing the ball and not sacrificing a stroke. If the shot is a risky one, there may be no point in taking a chance and ending up with a soaking.

You have to *help* the ball out of the water, whatever its lie. This entails choosing a club with plenty of loft and weight and taking up a stance well over the ball so that with the steeper swing you can get underneath it. Distance should certainly not be a significant consideration.

**Poor lies** It is often surprising exactly where a golf ball can end up, often appearing to have defied the laws of gravity. It may be balanced in the foliage of a small shrub or even caught in the branch of a tree. In the case of the latter there is little advice that can be given except to play the ball as best you can, making sure that you can get it far enough away from the tree to land on a reasonable piece of ground.

To play a ball balanced off the ground, place your hands down the handle as far as possible to insure a clean contact. As you have to strike up and into the ball, use a low, widened swing.

Another awkward position you may encounter is where the ball lies just below the surface, possibly in a divot that has been neglected or inadvertently dislodged. To play the ball, choose a lofted club and use a steep swing, with the ball fairly well back in the stance. The downward movement of the club-head should be more like a chopping action, the effect of which is to squirt the ball off on a fairly low trajectory.

The golden rule when you get yourself in trouble is to remain calm. There is nearly always a way out and by carefully weighing up the situation and working out your chances of success, you should be able to solve most problems without dropping too many strokes.

*When playing a raised ball, whether it is on the fringe of the rough (LEFT, TOP) or simply on a slope above your feet, it is wise to grip down the handle. (ABOVE). Not only does this reduce the length of the club, thus keeping the blade higher, but it also has the effect of calming the wrist action, which makes for a more accurate stroke.*

*From this awkward position—a poor lie on a down slope—where balance is essential, the legs are kept very still, the body turn is limited and the swing becomes more upright.*

*Here are three ways of attempting the near impossible (LEFT, ABOVE). At moments like these you should remember that for a one-stroke penalty you can drop the ball two club lengths clear!*

## Playing tactics

One of the great joys of golf is that the conditions under which you play and the situations which you face are never the same from one moment to the next. Every hole offers its own specific challenge; every shot is different to the previous one.

Having learned how to play the basic shots and how to cope with the demands of the course, there is another aspect of the game that is in many ways just as important if you want to improve your game and lower your handicap. It involves more of the mental approach – the tactical side – and it is very much reflected in how you overcome particular problems, take advantage of others and, faced with the many choices out on the course, make the right decisions.

Efforts to master this aspect of golf will only be successful when you are able to rely on your basic ability to play shots – but at the end of the day it can and does make the difference between winning and losing. On those occasions when, for one reason or another, your technique may be letting you down, it could well help you to survive what would otherwise turn out to be a disaster.

Playing tactics are developed over a period of time through much practice and experience, not only your own but also that of other golfers. In many respects it is a part of the game that you will spend the rest of your playing life learning about and adapting. While help and advice from others forms a major part of the process, it is not something that can be taught. It is very much to do with percentages, choosing from a set of options and developing a positive attitude, all of which must finally rest with the individual.

**Temperament** This is a vital factor in the playing of any sport and golf is no exception, particularly since there are so many elements to contend with during the course of a round.

There is your own mental and physical condition to cope with when you are out on the course. It may be that you do not feel in the right mood or are under the weather for whatever reason, but still have to play out a competition round.

The general conditions on the course may not be favorable. Perhaps it is cold and windy or raining on and off and this is playing havoc with your game. You may have ended up with a very bad lie in the rough or a bunker or suffered a particularly bad run of the ball on the green.

Possibly your technique is letting you down. You cannot get your swing going properly or your timing is fractionally out. You may have lost concentration on a crucial shot or been distracted in some way when lining up a vital putt.

When faced with these and other similar problems, it is all too easy to feel sorry for yourself, get depressed and then watch your whole game go to pieces. There is no doubt that when things start to run against you and you are feeling low, the situation gets increasingly worse – unless you do something about it. The only way out is to think and act positively. This, of course, is much easier said than done. But you must instill in yourself the necessary discipline to alter the situation and not ignore it in the hope that it will go away.

Take the positive attitude that every shot offers new hope. You may have made a complete hash of your drive off the tee and landed in thick rough off the fairway, but by concentrating on getting yourself back in the game, all you need is a good shot from there to restore your confidence. One well-hit stroke can make up for all the psychological damage caused by the previous bad ones.

When things do start to go wrong, stop for a moment or two and try to analyze why. It may be a slight fault in your tech-

*Even top professionals like Bernhard Langer sometimes miss putts, and when they do the tension may show (ABOVE). But the mark of a true professional is that they do not let such disappointments weaken their confidence.*

nique which, by concentrating on it immediately, you can put right on the spot. If the same fault returns, then it is more sensible to try to avoid further problems by getting around it some other way until you have finished the round and can go away and practice it.

If, for example, you are having trouble keeping your drives on the fairway, it may be worth trying a loftier wood or even a long iron and concentrating more on direction while sacrificing length. It could mean using an extra stroke at a long hole, but in the end this is bound to be less expensive than making a mess of a shot out of the rough.

Do not think of caution as being a negative approach. Recognizing your limitations and playing accordingly is, on the contrary, a very positive action. Hitting your way out of trouble may work on occasions, but there is little point in continuing to attack the ball when part of your basic technique is letting you down. Apart from the odd lucky shot, you are far more likely to aggravate the situation and plunge yourself into even greater despair.

It is far better to go on the defensive for a hole or two, build up your confidence again and then go back on the offensive. Even limited success at this stage will put you in a far better frame of mind.

**Shot selection** How well you perform on the golf couse will largely depend on how well you play your shots – but it will also depend on *what* shots you play. When selecting a shot you must pay particular attention to a range of relevant factors, such as the conditions at the time, the state of your own game, the situation at that stage of the match and what chances you feel you have of playing the shot successfully. Remember that there are times when you can go on the offensive, attack the ball and take a few calculated risks. On the other hand, there are times when you need to hold back, play safe and go for the less ambitious shot.

Take the first shot off the tee, for example. While the driver will give you the greatest distance down the fairway – and thus make it very tempting to get as close to the green as possible – you will have little or no control over the ball when it lands. Having got nearer the green, you may find to your horror that the ball has run into a bunker guarding it.

Think instead about taking a loftier wood – or even a long iron – and playing up short of the hazard to leave yourself a relatively simple short pitch or chip to the hole. In this way you can avoid the danger areas but still give yourself a chance of a par at that hole. Naturally, if you are confident that you *can* get the ball safely onto the green in one with a driver, then you should use it.

You may find, especially on the longer holes, that you cannot reach the green with your second shot, or, that if you try, you are likely to land in trouble. Having decided that you are going to sacrifice some distance, you are then in a position to go for direction and ball control. It is worth checking, too, as to whether there is a better spot to one side of the fairway from which to approach the green safely. If so, you should aim there and not for the center of the fairway.

Although you may find yourself in an awkward position after the first shot – perhaps with a tree between the ball and the green – it may still be possible by bending the ball to get it on the green. But if the green is a tight one and surrounded with hazards, then this could be a very risky shot to play. On reflection, the wiser shot is the one that takes the ball safely clear of trouble, although you should still aim to get as close to the green as possible. You have conceded a stroke on the fairway, it is true, but you may well have saved yourself one or two more getting back onto the green from a nearby hazard.

Having got safely to within striking distance of the green, you may still be faced with a decision as to how to play onto it. If there are any problem areas ahead and the hole is on that side of the green, then to aim directly for the hole could prove unprofitable. If you hit the ball too short, you may drop into a bunker, while even if you do reach the green you will have little control over the ball and it may overshoot.

In situations such as this, the decision for the less experienced player is again whether to go for the obvious shot or play safe – playing wide of the flag and keeping well away from the trouble-spots. This course of action could well prove to be the better choice in the long run.

There are literally thousands of examples that could be given to illustrate the question of shot selection. Your choice will be made a lot easier once you have gained enough experience to know, for example, the maximum distance you can send the ball with each club. It will also be a great advantage when you learn how to apply spin to the ball and what the different effects are. Equally, understanding how additional loft in the shot can be beneficial in certain cases and a disadvantage in others will prove essential.

What it all boils down to is knowing and accepting your own limitations as a

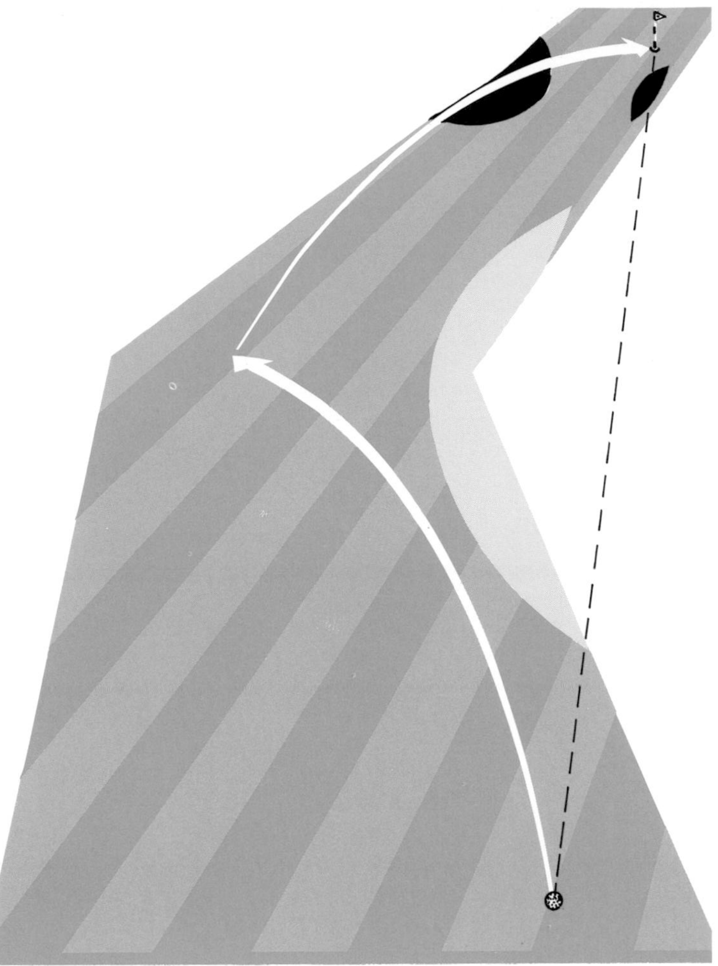

No matter how good you become as a player, there will be occasions when discretion is the better part of valor and there is no point in attempting the impossible. Sometimes it pays to play away from trouble and into position (ABOVE).

player when out on the course. If you are playing in a competitive match, that is not the time to start practicing to improve your game. Go for the shots you know you can play, unless you are faced with no other option. At least for the beginner the selection of shots available is limited anyway. The better you get, the wider the selection and often the harder the choice becomes.

**Competition play** This is the ultimate test of not only your ability as a player but also your character as a person. Under such conditions every flaw in your temperament and weakness in your technique is there for your opponent to take advantage of. At the same time, of course, you should be looking to exploit any opportunity that you are presented with to do the same. The player who recognizes such opportunities and makes the most of them will normally come out on top.

Sound judgment is the key to success in competition play, working out the percentage shots and knowing when to attack and when to defend. Although the principles are the same whatever type of competition you are playing in, there are certain tactics that suit one but should never be attempted for another.

In strokeplay, for example, every shot counts since it is the player with the least number of strokes who wins the day. Therefore every bad shot is recorded. In matchplay, a bad shot may lose you that particular hole, but a good one can just as easily win you the next. Thus, while in matchplay you might go for a very difficult shot which, if successful, would mean snatching the hole or even halving it, for the sake of that extra stroke on one hole in strokeplay it may well not be worth risking. Failure in the former case means losing a hole that you had virtually lost anyway, while missing the shot in strokeplay could cost you dearly if you put yourself in trouble and waste several more shots on that hole.

The differences in approach to these two basic types of competition are very marked. With strokeplay you are in effect playing just the course – trying to get around in the lowest number of strokes. Naturally at the end of the competition you hope to have fared better than anybody else, but it is not as though you are trying to match your opponent stroke for stroke. This, of course, is exactly what you *are* doing in matchplay, for the number of strokes taken at each hole is irrelevant as long as you take fewer strokes at more holes than your opponent.

All the time you are concentrating on your game, you must keep a check on how your opponent is playing. If he or she gets into trouble and you consider that their chances of getting out without any further problems are small, then you can afford to play safe with your next shot. Equally you may be forced to go for the poor percentage shot just to keep yourself in with a chance at that hole.

SECTION FIVE

# PLAYING WITHIN THE RULES

Playing golf is not just about mastering the techniques of striking the ball and sinking the putt in the minimum number of strokes. There is a universally accepted code of behavior for golfers that is designed to make the game enjoyable and satisfying for all concerned.

Apart from the basic rules of the game, which have been laid down and are administered by the United States Golf Association in conjunction with the Royal and Ancient Golf Club of St Andrews, there are established forms of competition for players to follow. There is also a handicapping system that enables players of different degrees of ability to compete fairly with each other.

These disciplines are there to make golf a worthwhile and successful pastime for all who wish to participate, whether on a friendly basis or in competition. But such rules and regulations that do exist can only be effective if everyone who goes out on the course understands and abides by the overall guidelines on courtesy. Without such behavior it would be impossible for so many to enjoy the facilities each golf course has to offer throughout the year.

## Etiquette

While it is easy, when you are on the course, to forget that there are many other golfers out there too, you must always give due consideration to them. After all, they have as much right to be out enjoying the facilities as you have.

It is understandable that at times you may be totally engrossed in your own game, such being the nature of the sport. But this is never an excuse to ignore the fact that people will be following up behind, wanting to get on with their own match. Courtesy on the course, therefore, is a very important and necessary part of everyone's game – from the beginner right through to the expert.

Etiquette goes hand in hand with safety and many of the rules relating to this aspect of golf have been specifically designed to avoid unnecessary aggravation and dangerous play. You therefore ignore this subject at your peril, not only from fellow golfers and club officials but also from the golf ball.

**Care for others** There is nothing more infuriating when playing a round and getting into full swing than to be held up by the match in front. Thus, whenever possible you must avoid unnecessarily delaying those players following you.

You should never waste time looking for a lost ball when there is a match directly behind you. If you cannot find your ball after a reasonable length of time – a ball is deemed lost after five minutes' search – then you must wave through the players following on and renew your search afterward. If you lose a clear hole on the match ahead, you should be prepared to allow any game waiting behind you to play through.

Always check the rules of the club at which you are playing, since there may be certain variations. As a general principle, however, two-ball matches always take precedence over any other form of match. This means anyone playing this type of match should be allowed to pass through a three- or four-ball match. Golfers playing on their own must give way to everyone else on the course.

Having completed a hole, players should leave the green as quickly as possible to enable the match behind to play onto it. The golden rule when on the course is never to play a shot until the people ahead are out of range. This is why, if your particular match is slower than the one behind, frustration can quickly creep in – and unfortunately this can in some cases lead to potentially dangerous situations as those in line behind grow more and more impatient.

Concentration is an essential part of play and no golfer welcomes distractions, however small, when preparing for and playing a shot. This means you should never stand near to or directly in the line of sight of someone who is preparing to take a shot. You should also remain still and quiet and not start talking, shuffling about or lifting clubs out of your bag.

From a safety point of view as well, you should never stand anywhere in front of the player taking the shot or directly behind. There have, sadly, been some very nasty accidents where golfers have been struck by club-heads and balls. Although it is the responsibility of all players to make sure there is no potential danger when they take their shot, the fault lies just as much with those onlookers who have not taken the necessary precautions.

One point to remember at the start of each hole is that those waiting to take their tee shot should never tee up their ball until the player who "has the honour" has struck the ball.

Should your ball be in the way of someone playing a shot – and this is normally more likely to happen on the green – you will be required to mark the spot and lift your ball. You cannot make a mark on the ground, but should always use a small disk that will not distract the person whose turn it is to play. The disk is placed directly behind your ball.

You may possibly be required to move this marker out of the line of shot. In this case, you will have to measure from the original position of the ball with the blade of your putter, in a line perpendicular to the target line. In extreme cases you may have to move the marker more than one blade's length from the original spot. When the other player has taken the shot, you simply reverse the procedure with the blade of the putter to reestablish the correct original position of your ball.

**Care for the course** Consideration for other golfers is not just a matter of showing them due courtesy when playing. It is equally important to show due respect for the course itself so that all who follow can get as much satisfaction from their round as you do.

This principle applies first at the tee and, in particular, the collection of tee pegs after the first shot has been played. When the teeing area is very wet, try to avoid walking about too much. With the number of feet that necessarily have to tread on it in the course of a day, the ground can get very chewed up and make the job of taking a firm stance almost impossible. Furthermore, you should never practice your swing on the tee unless you are actually about to tee off. When on the fairway, always insure you replace any divots made with the club-head.

Should you be unfortunate enough to put your ball in a bunker, do not just walk away after you have hit the ball out. There will be a few footprints and a large strike mark in the sand where the ball lay. These should be smoothed over with either the club-head or the sole of your shoe. On some courses, a special rake may be provided near the bunker to make the necessary repairs.

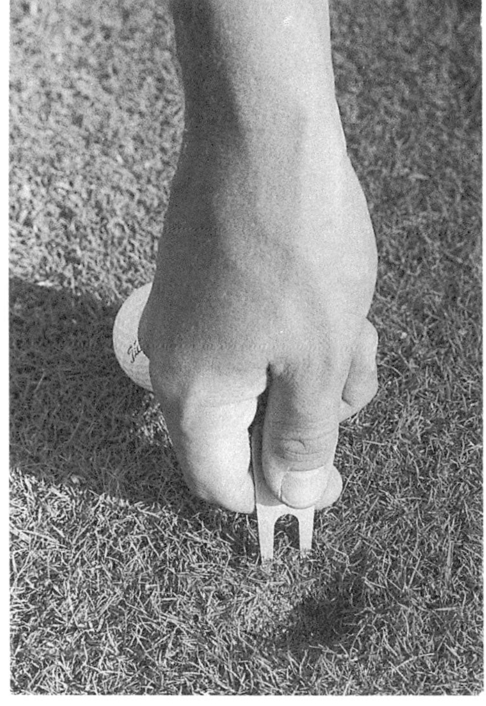

*Always use a pitchfork (LEFT) to repair any pitchmarks made in the surface of the green. After carefully lifting up the impacted turf, tap the area flat with the sole of your putter.*

The most vulnerable part of any golf course is the green. Here particular attention should be paid to leave the turf in the same condition as you would wish to find it. All clubs, bags and trolleys must be left off the edge of the green, although you will want to have them as near to hand as possible. You should also tread carefully when walking across the turf and not scuff or drag your feet.

If you happen to make any pitchmarks in the surface of the green, never just tread them in with your shoe. If you try to flatten them in this way, the grass underneath will rot and leave a nasty mark on the surface. To repair this damage, you should use a small pitchfork, which you can get from the professional's shop. Lift up the damaged turf carefully and replace the disturbed piece in its original position.

The holes themselves are particularly vulnerable, since careless feet can easily damage the sides. You should never stand right up to the hole when removing or replacing the flagstick or when you are taking your ball out. Constant pressure from feet will eventually create a ridge around the lip of the hole and play havoc with that final putt. Equally, you must not lean on your putter when removing the ball since this will mark the turf.

## Forms of play

There is a wide variety of games and matches you can engage in on the golf course, such as matchplay, strokeplay and Stableford. Within these types there are also many different combinations, depending on the number of players participating and the number of balls used. The basic types are as follows:

*Singles:* one person playing along with or against another, each using their own ball.

*Foursome:* two people playing along with or against two others, each side using one ball and playing alternate shots.

*Three-ball:* three people playing along with or against each other, each player using a separate ball.

*Four-ball:* two people playing with or against two others, each side counting the score of the better ball of the two.

Each type of game or match has its own handicap allowance. These are discussed in the section on handicapping (see page 218).

**Matchplay** This form of competition is played on a hole-by-hole basis. The winner is the player or players to have won more holes than there are holes left to play on the given course. Each hole is won by the side taking the least number of strokes at that hole. Where the players at the finish of a hole have played the same number of strokes, that hole is halved. In a handicap match, however, the lower net score wins the hole. If the players have, by the end of the match, won the same number of holes, then the game is halved and called "all square." However, if a result is required then a sudden death play-off is used to decide the result. Matchplay can be in the form of singles, foursomes or four-ball.

**Strokeplay** As the name implies, this form of competition is played on a stroke-by-stroke basis over a predetermined number of rounds. The winner is the player who completes the round or rounds in the lowest number of strokes. The handicap is deducted from the total to give a net result. Strokeplay can be in the form of singles, foursomes or four-ball.

**Stableford** With this form of competition, the net score after deducting any handicap allowance is compared with the par for each hole in turn. Scoring is on a points basis, where two points are awarded if the net score is level par and an extra point awarded for every stroke less than par for that hole. For a net score of one over par, one point is scored. If more strokes are taken, no points are scored. Stableford can be in the form of singles, foursomes or four-ball – and more rarely greensomes.

One reason for the popularity of this type of competition is that while it rewards those who do particularly well at a specific hole, it does not penalize too heavily someone who fares badly. So even the most erratic golfer does have the chance to return a reasonable score at the end of a round.

**Greensome foursome** This form of competition is played in pairs. After both players on one side have played a tee shot, they have to decide which ball to continue playing with. The second shot is then played by the person whose ball is picked up. All other shots played on that hole are then taken alternately.

**Texas scramble** The great advantage of this type of competition, which is becoming increasingly popular, is that even the worst of players can join in with much better golfers and still feel they are contributing to the round. Basically each player takes his or her own first shot. Whoever's ball ends up in the best situation, all the other players then play their next shot from that position. This continues for every shot until the hole is completed.

## Par for the course

Each hole on a golf course is given a par figure, which is estimated on the basis of the length of that hole. By adding together the par figures for each of the 18 holes, the "par for the course" is arrived at. The par figure allows for two putt shots on each green and however many a player will need to reach that green, based entirely on yardage for that specific hole.

This means that a par 3 hole is one that a good golfer would be expected to reach in one shot from the tee. This is estimated to be anything up to 228m (250yd). A par 4 hole is one longer than 228m (250yd) and up to 434m (475yd) long, where two shots should put a good player on the green. A par 5 hole is one more than 434m (475yd) long, which is assumed normally to be beyond the reach of a golfer in two shots – and therefore three are allowed.

Occasionally you may come across a par 6 hole. This is very rare and there is no determining distance for this type of hole.

**Standard Scratch Score** This method of establishing an overall par for the course was introduced to identify the relative degree of difficulty of individual courses. It is calculated on the total length of the 18 holes and not the total par figures for those holes.

In some cases the SSS figure is higher, where holes are on the long side within the par limit, while in other cases the SSS may be lower, where holes are on the short side within the par limit. For example, the majority of par 4 holes on one course may be in excess of 365m (400yd), while on another course they may be on average about 275m (300yd). Therefore the fact that the holes on the first course are longer, and so playing to par more difficult, will show up if the SSS figure is known. The assessment for total par is based on the following figures:

| **Total Length of course** | | **Assessed SSS** |
|---|---|---|
| Meters | (Yards) | |
| 3659–3840 | (4001–4200) | 60 |
| 3841–4023 | (4201–4400) | 61 |
| 4024–4206 | (4401–4600) | 62 |
| 4207–4389 | (4601–4800) | 63 |
| 4390–4572 | (4801–5000) | 64 |
| 4573–4755 | (5001–5200) | 65 |
| 4756–4983 | (5201–5450) | 66 |
| 4984–5212 | (5451–5700) | 67 |
| 5213–5441 | (5701–5950) | 68 |
| 5442–5669 | (5951–6200) | 69 |
| 5670–5852 | (6201–6400) | 70 |
| 5853–6035 | (6401–6600) | 71 |
| 6036–6218 | (6601–6800) | 72 |
| 6219–6401 | (6801–7000) | 73 |
| 6402–6584 | (7001–7200) | 74 |

Although these general figures have been worked out on an average basis over a 12-month period to take into account the varying conditions through the year, each course is also personally assessed by a team of officials from its county golfing authority.

The job of these officials is to inspect each course, taking into account such things as its situation, whether coastal or inland; the type and normal conditions of the terrain; the overall lanscape; the width of the fairways and the sizes of the greens; and also the number and siting of various hazards, such as water, bunkers and "out of bounds" areas. These and other relevant aspects are looked at in conjunction with the official assessment based purely on the length of the course and the SSS figure may well be adjusted accordingly.

## Scoring terms

On the course, certain terms are used to indicate the number of strokes taken on each hole. When these exceed the par for the hole, the score would be referred to as one over par, two over par, and so on. Where the hole has been played in under par, the following are used:

**Birdie** When the hole is played in one stroke less than par for that hole – for example, a par 4 in three.
**Eagle** When the hole is played in two strokes less than par for that hole – for example, a par 5 in three.
**Albatross** When the hole is played in three strokes less than par for that hole – for example, a par 5 in two or even a par 4 "holed in one."

## FURTHER READING

**GOLF MAGAZINE'S SHORTCUTS TO BETTER GOLF**
Edited by Lew Fishman and Golf Magazine's editors
Published by Harper & Row 1979

**GOLF MANUAL**
Alex Hay
Published by Faber & Faber 1980

**GOLF RULES IN PICTURES**
U.S.G.A.
(New Revised Edition)
Published by Putnam Publishing Group 1984

**JACK NICKLAUS PLAYING LESSONS**
Jack Nicklaus and Ken Bowden
Published by Golf Digest 1981

**JACK NICKLAUS THE FULL SWING IN PHOTOS**
Jack Nicklaus and Ken Bowden
Published by Golf Digest 1984

**JACK NICKLAUS LESSON TEE**
Jack Nicklaus and Ken Bowden
Published by Simon & Schuster 1978

**GOLF RULES EXPLAINED**
Peter Dobereiner
Published by David & Charles 1984

**HOW TO BECOME A COMPLETE GOLFER**
Bob Toski and Jim Flick
Published by Golf Digest 1984

**BOB TOSKI'S COMPLETE GUIDE TO BETTER GOLF**
Bob Toski and Dick Aultman
Published by Atheneum 1980

**GOLFERS HANDBOOK**
Edited by Percy Huggins
Published by International Publishing Services

# INDEX

The page numbers in *italic* refer to the illustrations and captions.

## A



## B

# L



# M



# N

# R



# S

## T

## U

## V

## W

# PICTURE CREDITS

Unless otherwise indicated, all photographs are by Ian Howes.

10 Phil Sheldon: 14 John Hesletine: 16 John Hesletine: 18/9 John Hesletine: 20/1 John Hesletine: 22/3 John Hesletine: 24/5 John Hesletine: 26/7 John Hesletine: 28/9 John Hesletine: 30 John Hesletine: 32 John Hesletine: 33 (top and inset) William Martin Audio Visual: 33 Dunlop Slazenger Ltd: 34/5 John Hesletine: 36/7 John Hesletine: 36 (inset) David Muscroft: 38/9 John Hesletine: 40/1 John Hesletine: 42/3 John Hesletine: 44/5 Brent Moore: 69 Brent Moore: 70/1 Brent Moore: 72/3 Brent Moore: 74/5 Brent Moore: 76/7 Brent Moore: 78/9 Brent Moore: 80/1 Brent Moore: 96/7 Brent Moore; 112 Brent Moore: 114/5 (top) Brent Moore: 148/9 Brent Moore: 157 Brent Moore: 192/3 George Herringshaw: 194 E.D. Lacey: 209 All-Action Photographic.

# ACKNOWLEDGEMENTS

The special thanks of the publisher are due to the La Manga Club, without whose generous assistance this book would not have been possible, and to Dunlop Slazenger Ltd.